TOURING
COLORADO
HOT SPRINGS

The pools and ponds at Valley View Hot Springs are open to overnight guests 24 hours a day.
SCOTT RAPPOLD - COURTESY VALLEY VIEW

TOURING
COLORADO
HOT SPRINGS

THIRD EDITION

Susan Joy Paul

FALCONGUIDES

GUILFORD, CONNECTICUT

To my dad, Edward Joseph Paul, and his adventurer's heart,
and to my mom, Jane Lillian Clifford, and her writer's soul—
there's a bit of you both in here.

FALCONGUIDES®

An imprint of The Rowman & Littlefield Publishing Group, Inc.
4501 Forbes Blvd., Ste. 200
Lanham, MD 20706
www.rowman.com

Falcon and FalconGuides are registered trademarks and Make Adventure Your
Story is a trademark of The Rowman & Littlefield Publishing Group, Inc.

Distributed by NATIONAL BOOK NETWORK

British Library Cataloguing-in-Publication Information available

Library of Congress Cataloging-in-Publication Data available

ISBN 978-1-4930-2915-0 (paperback)
ISBN 978-1-4930-2916-7 (e-book)

∞™ The paper used in this publication meets the minimum requirements of
American National Standard for Information Sciences—Permanence of Paper for
Printed Library Materials, ANSI/NISO Z39.48-1992.

Printed in the United States of America

The author and The Rowman & Littlefield Publishing Group, Inc. assume no liability
for accidents happening to, or injuries sustained by, readers who engage in the
activities described in this book.

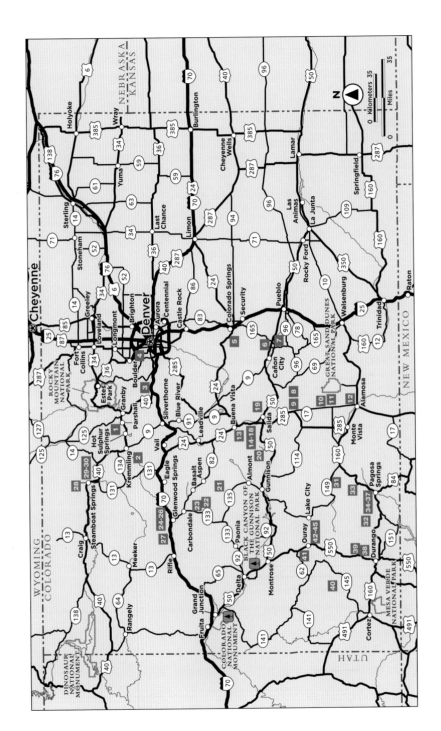

CONTENTS

The Hot Springs

ACKNOWLEDGMENTS

I couldn't write a word without the support of my family. Thank you for being so understanding when I'm up to my ears in research and writing, and unavailable for everything else: Jane Clifford, Priscilla Paul, Carolyn McNeil, Alison Milligan, Melissa Clifford, Joshua Levesque, Kimmy Flack, and Garrett Schaller.

I wouldn't have many of the stunning photos in this book if it weren't for my friend, fellow author, and photographer Stewart M. Green, who sacrificed a lot of weekends to tour the hot springs with me for this book.

I shouldn't take for granted all the anonymous hot springs soakers who shared the pools, ponds, tubs, and baths with me on my tour of the Colorado hot springs. Thank you for the company!

I can't thank enough all the commercial hot springs owners, management, and staff who took the time to answer my questions and provide me with access to the hot springs: Heather Austin, Nick Baranek, Donnie Bautista, Chandelle Bernard, Doug Bishop, Jeanine Boecker, Elizabeth Brath, Michael Bush, Craig Cardwell, Tracie Cardwell, Theresa Casey, Kelly Castellano, Samantha Cooper, Emma Copp, Katie Craig, Corinne Diemoz-Deraddo, Gill Engles, Jeremy Gilley, Mandy Golden, Matthew Hall, Robin Hall, Carly Harmon, Ryan Hein, Ian Henderson, Molly Jacober, Vince Kaminski, Randi Kerns, Mindy Kinsella, Sally Kloman, Mary Jane Kuboske, Erica Larson, Lindsey Leavell, Pete Leavell, Missy Lee, Shane Lucero, James Mac, Conner Mather, Patrick McCannon, Lee Mills, Meredith Ogilby, Harold Palmer, Judy Palmer, Scott Peterson, Tom Poole, Robin "Rosie" Rosenberg, Donna Roth, Brandon Salazar, Enid Shaw-Richards, Angie Shrock, Gabriela Silva, Lora Slawitschka, Sharyle Solis, Donna Spesshardt, Patsy Steele, Joe Stepan, Josh Vincent, Lauren Wallace, Patty Walters, Samantha Watson, Wendy Wilkinson, Erin Young, and Maria Ziemba.

And finally, I won't ever be able to thank enough my acquisitions editor, David Legere; production editor, Lynn Zelem; map manager, Melissa Baker; copyeditor, Kathy Brock; layout artist, Melissa Evarts; and publisher, Falcon Guides/The Rowman & Littlefield Publishing Group, for all your hard work—and patience.

—Susan Joy Paul

Facing page: Snowy mountaintops and the Colorado River provide the backdrop at Hot Sulphur Springs Resort & Spa, Hot Sulphur Springs. STEWART M. GREEN

INTRODUCTION

Welcome to the hot and steamy world of Colorado hot springs. Ours is a big state with many hot springs, all ready and waiting to accommodate every soaker, swimmer, and steamer willing to make the journey.

If you grew up here and spent weekends at local hot springs with your family, prepare to discover some new places. If you live in this state but have never been to a hot spring, you're in for a treat, and you won't have to go far! In this book, you'll find dozens of hot springs where you can spend an afternoon, a weekend, or longer—all within a few hours' drive of your home. If you live outside the state, you can use this book to plan your Colorado hot springs vacation and choose one hot spring to visit, or make a tour of it across the state. If you received this book as a gift and don't know a single thing about hot springs or why you would want to go to one, you're in luck! There are different soaks for different folks, and when it comes to Colorado hot springs, there's something for everyone. In this book, I'll introduce you to more than forty-five of my favorites and help you select the hot spring that's just right for you.

Colorado hot springs satisfy people of all sizes and shapes, ages, persuasions, interests, and abilities. Whether you're traveling alone, with a partner, or with your family or a group, there's a hot spring in Colorado that's perfect for your needs. There are cozy private tubs and baths for romantic getaways, big family fun centers with pools for moms, dads, and all the kids, and sprawling resorts and ranches for big groups, clubs, and corporate retreats. For the little ones, there are baby and toddler hot springs pools; for swimmers, there are lap pools, play pools, and diving pools. There are hot spring pools with slides, volleyball nets, basketball hoops, fountains, toys, and waterfalls. There are even a couple of hot springs pools with inflatable obstacle courses and climbing walls! There are therapeutic soaking pools, too, indoor and outdoor hot pots, pools, and ponds with steam rooms, saunas, solariums, vapor caves, or views of the Rocky Mountains. Some are calm and some have jets, some are formed in concrete or lined in river rock, while others are simply craters in the earth with mineral springs bubbling up in a hot bath of nature's bounty. While some of the pools require you to don a bathing suit, naturism is the norm at plenty of them, with indoor soaking tubs for the modest and outdoor community pools for those happy to bare all in the Colorado sunshine. Many of the commercial hot springs sites offer massage and spa treatments, body rubs and facial scrubs, waxing, wraps, and reflexology. And while you can drive to most of the hot springs, a few will appeal to hikers and campers, with short and long hikes required to bathe in their waters. Even the wheelchair-bound can partake in the hot springs of Colorado, as many facilities are ADA-compliant and several have hydraulic lifts from chair to pool, pool-ready chairs, and ramps to accommodate them. For young and old and all ages in between,

Facing page: The Mother Spring in Pagosa Springs is the deepest hot spring on the planet and the source of all that hot water at The Springs Resort & Spa. STEWART M. GREEN

for those seeking relief for sore muscles from their backcountry adventures or mental weariness from too much work, whether you come to play or for the peace, there's a hot spring for you in Colorado.

So grab a towel and a bottle of water, and let's get started on our tour of the hot springs. There's one in here that's just for you and I know we're going to find it!

HOT SPRINGS GEOLOGY:
WHERE DOES ALL THAT HOT WATER COME FROM?

Before we head off on the tour, you're probably wondering where hot springs came from. How did they get here? They didn't just fall out of the sky—or did they? Actually, in a way, they did!

Hot springs are a result of the natural cycle of water as it moves over and through the earth's crust. When surface water from oceans and lakes evaporates through the effects of sun and wind, it's carried into the atmosphere as vapor. As the vapor cools it precipitates and falls to the ground, in the form of rain, sleet, or snow—and in Colorado, often hail or graupel. Some of this moisture is absorbed into the subsoil and ends up as part of an aquifer, fluid trapped in underground reservoirs of wet gravel. Where there are no impermeable layers of clay or bedrock to inhibit its downward progress, the water may filter down and become heated by molten rock, deep beneath the earth's surface. The heated water rises, seeking out natural fault lines and fissures, and if it finds an opening, it emerges from the ground as a hot spring.

Some hot springs referenced in this book developed less naturally, as a result of wells drilled into the earth. In some cases the driller was looking for oil and happened to tap into water instead. Other wells were intentionally drilled into known geothermal zones with the express intent of tapping the hot water.

A hot spring can suddenly appear—or disappear—due to movement beneath the earth, and that's why it's so tough to get an accurate count of exactly how many there are in Colorado or anywhere else. Appendix A provides the latest known listing of all hot springs in the state.

A natural hot spring site that you visit today has probably been around for at least a few centuries, while man-made thermal flows haven't been around nearly as long. But no matter how it was brought to the surface, all hot spring water has absorbed some minerals from the underground rocks. Sulfur, copper, iron, sodium, lithium, and phosphorous are commonly found in hot spring water, to the delight of soakers who value those minerals and the potential health benefits.

HISTORY OF COLORADO HOT SPRINGS

Ute, Arapaho, Cheyenne, and other Native Americans soaked at the hot springs for hundreds of years before white settlers came into the picture. Growth into these areas was fueled by mining activity and railroad expansion, and during the 1800s, many hot springs were privatized and developed as destinations for those in search of potential health benefits. Resorts and sanitariums grew up around the waters, where people

Facing page: The hot spring water source at Waunita Hot Springs is nearby 11,465-foot Tomichi Dome. STEWART M. GREEN

bathed in—and often drank from—the hot springs, with hopes of curing everything from rheumatism to tuberculosis. Many of these old structures were lost to fires and sometimes floods, and interest waned with the advent of modern medicine.

After about a century and a half of ups and downs, the hot springs of Colorado have reinvented themselves with the addition of lodging, fitness centers, spas, massage services, balneotherapy, and salons, all in line with a general move toward better health, natural healing, and improved quality of life. This trend is very appealing to the new breed of hot springs enthusiasts, and the hot springs are flourishing in response.

On my second tour of the Colorado hot springs in 2017, their popularity was even more evident, and some are routinely booked to capacity. Before you make plans for a big trip to a hot spring, call to make sure they can accommodate you.

BALNEOLOGY, HYDROTHERAPY, AND HOT SPRINGS

Colorado's hot springs have always been celebrated as places to relax, recover, and rejuvenate. Years ago some of them operated as sanitariums, and many were go-to spots for everything that ailed a person, from general malaise to skin disorders, mental illness, and serious disease.

While they may not be the cure-all they were once believed to be, hot springs are still sought out by many people who swear by their healing properties and health benefits. Balneotherapy and hydrotherapy, or soaking in mineral waters—often accompanied by massage, gentle stretching, and joint manipulation—are offered at many Colorado hot springs for a fee.

Above: SunWater Spa and nearby SunMountain Center in Manitou Springs embody a culture of wellness that's reflected in soaking, therapies, massage, yoga, food, farming, lodging, and retreats. COURTESY SUNWATER SPA

Facing page: The Historic Wiesbaden Hot Springs Spa & Lodgings is the oldest commercial spring in Ouray, a town nearly bursting with hot springs. STEWART M. GREEN

While this book does not intend to make any medical claims about the benefits of soaking at a hot spring, you are encouraged to further research the subject of balneology. Soaking in a hot bath has long been prescribed as a remedy for soothing the symptoms of physical and mental overexertion, and doing so in a hot mineral bath, and especially outdoors in the brilliant Colorado sunshine with views of the Rocky Mountains, certainly seems to improve one's demeanor and promote an overall sense of well-being. You may not be healed, but you will probably feel a lot better.

Minerals common to Colorado hot springs and believed to offer health benefits include, but are not limited to:

❊ Arsenic	❊ Fluoride	❊ Nitrogen
❊ Barium	❊ Iron	❊ Phosphate
❊ Bicarbonate	❊ Lead	❊ Potassium
❊ Boron	❊ Lithium	❊ Selenium
❊ Cadmium	❊ Magnesium	❊ Silica
❊ Calcium	❊ Manganese	❊ Silver
❊ Chloride	❊ Mercury	❊ Sodium
❊ Chromium	❊ Molybdenum	❊ Sulphate
❊ Copper	❊ Nitrate	❊ Zinc

Some commercial sites regularly test and publish the mineral content found in their hot springs, and that data is compiled in Appendix B.

COMMERCIAL AND WILD SPRINGS: WHAT'S THE DIFFERENCE?

While most of Colorado's hot springs started out as wild springs—remember, some were intentionally drilled for commercial use—most of them have been developed by private owners and are now commercial hot springs. So, what's the difference?

Commercial hot springs are privately owned, usually by individuals, although the Ouray Hot Springs Pool & Fitness Center is owned by the City of Ouray. They are for-profit and charge a fee for entrance. Most hot springs accept credit cards, but some—like Strawberry Park Hot Springs—do not, so call ahead and see if you need to bring some cash or your checkbook.

Daily admittance to a commercial hot spring can vary from about $10 to nearly $1,000, depending on the site and the services provided. For example, some commercial hot springs offer lodging and their pools are for guests only, so the cost to soak will be much higher than a simple day pass. However, many hot springs that offer lodging are also open to "day-soakers," or people who just want to come for a soak or a swim and not an overnight stay. If you want to know whether a hot spring accepts day-soakers or not, check out the planning section at the beginning of each chapter under Rules and look for the phrase "day-soakers welcome," which indicates there is lodging available but soaking is also open to nonguests; "day-soaker facility" which

Facing page: Guests of The Historic Wiesbaden Hot Springs Spa & Lodgings can enjoy a therapeutic massage in the vapor cave. STEWART M. GREEN

indicates there is no lodging and so the site is for day-soakers only; or "no day-soakers, guests only" for sites where soaking is reserved for overnight guests.

Within the group of commercial hot springs are several vacation rental hot springs, which are homes, cabins, or ranches available for reservation, where you have the entire rental and associated hot spring pool to yourself.

Although commercial hot springs are owned and operated by private entities, the hot mineral water you enjoy so much is a natural product, and so a lot of work goes into keeping these sites clean while allowing the natural properties and benefits of the waters to remain. Commercial sites drain, clean, and refill their pools regularly, and many of them have a continuous flow of fresh mineral water, making them cleaner than traditional swimming pools. Few use chlorine or any chemicals at all, and the larger sites go to great lengths to filter their water before it enters a pool. Discoloration in a pool and even "floaties" in the water are caused by minerals and to be expected. These are not chlorine-saturated city pools, so if your hot spring pool has a bit of rust-colored minerals near the drain, or granules, flakes, and chips in the water, don't complain to the management. Those minerals are what make the hot springs special. In addition to regular daily or weekly cleaning, some sites close down for a few days every year for a more thorough, top-to-bottom cleaning of the entire facility.

Many commercial hot springs have newsletters, so if you become a fan of a particular establishment, you can sign up for email notices about pool news, changes in hours, closures, and special events. Most of them offer annual passes as well, so if you feel like you might become a regular, a pass might save you some money in the long run, and you'll be more inclined to visit the hot springs more often.

Unlike commercial hot springs, wild springs are free. They lie along rivers and in national forests, wilderness area, on Bureau of Land Management (BLM) and county land, and while you can visit them unfettered by the many rules of commercial springs, wild springs require even more tender care. They are fewer, smaller, generally unmaintained, and prone to abuse and overuse. A wild spring is not a party zone. If you visit one, follow the rules of the land area.

Make your visits to wild springs few and far between. Treat the waters and surrounding area gently, and don't foul the water or allow your pet to foul it either. Keep food and drinks away, and if you pack anything into camp nearby—food wrappers, cans, or personal items—pack it out when you leave. Don't leave anything behind to spoil the beauty of a wild spring, the habitat of the plants and animals that make the hot springs their home, or the experience of the next visitor to the wild spring.

CLOTHING OPTIONAL: HOT SPRINGS AND NATURISM

Clothing-optional hot springs may not be the norm in Colorado, but they're not the exception either. In fact, twenty-two of the forty-five-plus hot springs sites in this book have clothing-optional areas, hours, or days, or they don't require suits at all, all the time. At hot springs that combine clothing-required and clothing-optional soaking areas, the two are segregated.

Facing page: You can often grab a solo soak at Penny Hot Springs, a wild spring north of Redstone. STEWART M. GREEN

Use your best judgment when deciding whether to go clothed or au naturel at a wild spring like South Canyon Hot Springs. STEWART M. GREEN

Orvis Hot Springs in Ridgway is a popular clothing-optional commercial hot springs site in Colorado. STEWART M. GREEN

Clothing-optional "naturism" is generally restricted to soaking areas only, so you won't see people roaming the hallways in the buff, and respectful behavior is demanded. As one commercial hot spring puts it, "Be nude, not lewd." In fact, some clothing-optional hot springs disallow public displays of affection of any kind, specifically in communal areas, and inappropriate behavior at any of these hot springs will most likely get you thrown out on your bare keister.

If you're new to sans-suit soaking and want to give it a try, you can start by going solo in a private bath, then try it with a good friend or partner. On your next outing, opt for a gender-specific communal bath, and bring a couple of friends along. Soon enough you'll find yourself quite comfortable at an indoor or outdoor, coed, clothing-optional facility, wondering what all that fuss in your head was about, anyway—or not. After all, it's optional.

You can easily discover Colorado's clothing-optional pools, tubs, baths, and ponds by browsing the planning section at the beginning of each chapter for the phrase "clothing is optional," "clothing is recommended," or "clothing is required" under Rules.

HOT SPRINGS SAFETY AND PROTOCOL

Abide by a code of conduct and these simple rules to stay safe at the hot springs and ensure you're welcomed back.

❋ People who are pregnant, have high blood pressure, or who are on medication or under a doctor's care should speak to their physician before soaking at a hot spring or entering a vapor cave.

Calmness is key at some hot springs, such as Joyful Journey Hot Springs Spa in the San Luis Valley. STEWART M. GREEN

* Use caution when introducing elderly people and children to the hot springs—both should stay clear of very hot waters. Many hot springs offer kiddie pools with waters of about 98°, or body temperature, to ensure that tender skin is safe from scalding.

* If you're traveling to the hot springs from sea level, you may experience some mild altitude sickness. The symptoms usually wear off soon enough, and you can stave them off by drinking enough water, eating, resting, and taking an over-the-counter pain reliever. If you're concerned about it, speak to your doctor first about the best way to treat altitude sickness, should it occur.

* Freshwater should be consumed prior to visiting the hot springs to ensure proper hydration, and you'll want to keep a plastic or metal bottle of water close at hand while soaking to keep you hydrated and also to cool you off from the inside out, as needed.

* Don't bring glass containers to the hot springs. One broken bottle can shut down a pool for days.

* Shower before you soak to remove any chemicals and impurities from your body's surface—such as deodorants and perfumes—so you don't introduce them into the fresh mineral water. Rinse completely before entering the water. Post-soak showering is up to you; many people prefer to leave the minerals from the water on their skin for a time. All commercial hot springs have showers for your use; some of them utilize hot spring water and most of them ask that you shower first.

Many hot springs, like Cottonwood Hot Springs Inn & Spa, Buena Vista, are perfect for relaxing, meditation, renewal—and soaking. STEWART M. GREEN

Radium Hot Springs is the closest wild spring to the Denver area and popular year-round.
SUSAN JOY PAUL

* Remove all silver jewelry, or be prepared to buff out the tarnish.

* Do not soak while under the influence of alcohol or drugs; you could become dizzy, dehydrated, nauseous, and could even pass out and drown. Most hot springs have strict rules against their use in the pools and sometimes on the entire property. For this reason, commercial hot springs that serve alcohol may have a drink limit.

* Some hot springs have a designated area for smoking cigarettes and/or marijuana, usually downwind from the pools. Don't assume you can smoke in your car, your room, or anywhere else at a hot spring. Ask at the front desk and follow the rules.

* Although some hot springs tout their waters as potable, drinking hot spring water—especially water in which others are bathing—is not recommended. The exception is water that has been bottled or provided from a tap that expressly states it's suitable for human consumption.

* Most hot springs suggest soaking for 10 minutes at a time and then cooling off. You can cover yourself with a towel in the winter—and in the summer if you prefer to sweat—but the important thing is to get out of the hot water and cool off for a bit before getting back in. You should also limit your overall time in a hot spring.

* Get out of the hot spring water immediately if you feel dizzy, nauseous, or faint, and seek assistance.

* In the event of a thunderstorm, most commercial outdoor hot springs sites require you to get out of the water. At wild hot springs, use your best judgment.

* Follow the rules of each hot spring in regard to pets, food, and any other restrictions.

* Clothing-optional facilities in particular tend to have strict rules against cell phones and cameras, so if that's the case, leave them in the car.

* Pick up after yourself, at commercial sites as well as undeveloped ones. If you're hiking out to a hot spring, be prepared to carry out all your trash.

* Some hot springs foster a quiet, relaxed atmosphere, even reserving special areas for adults only, while others are made especially for water play. In either case, respect the rights of others, and be courteous in your behavior. Running, screaming, spitting, foul language, and fistfights are prohibited at most hot springs, and soakers who persist in this type of behavior should not expect to be welcomed back or even allowed to remain. Have a good time, but let everybody else have a good time too.

Outdoor Jacuzzis at Indian Hot Springs are enclosed for privacy. STEWART M. GREEN

HOW TO USE THIS GUIDE

With all the hot springs out there, how do you decide which ones are for you? This book is organized to make choosing your hot spring easy.

Since your first consideration is probably location, the hot springs are grouped into five regions of the state: the Front Range, San Luis Valley, Central Rockies, Northern Rockies, and Southwest Colorado.

If you live in the Front Range's Denver area, the four closest hot springs are located in Hot Sulphur Springs, Radium, Idaho Springs, and Eldorado Springs. These are good choices if your trip plans include the metro area or Rocky Mountain National Park. If you're farther south, in the Colorado Springs or Cañon City area, three Front Range hot springs are nearby in Manitou Springs, Penrose, and Florence. These are great choices for trips to the Royal Gorge area.

Traveling southwest of the Front Range is the San Luis Valley. The five hot springs here are all situated along CO 17 between Villa Grove and Alamosa. This is a beautiful area bordered by the San Juan Mountains to the west and the Sangre de Cristo Mountains to the east. The Great Sand Dunes National Park & Preserve is nearby, and the lower Arkansas River beckons for kayaking and white water rafting.

Venturing to the center of the state, we come to the fifteen Central Rockies hot springs. These are spread out from Glenwood Springs to Buena Vista and Salida to Gunnison, and all are accessible on major roadways from the Denver and Colorado Springs areas. The exception is Conundrum Hot Springs, a 17-mile round-trip hike that starts at a trailhead near Aspen. The Central Rockies are a good location if your

Facing page and above: Rico Hot Springs is on private property and is not legally accessible to soakers. STEWART M. GREEN

Juniper Hot Springs in northwest Colorado was closed in 2017 due to vandalism, but soakers would love to see the place renovated and reopened. PHOTOS BY STEWART M. GREEN

The author soaks up the sunshine at Ouray Hot Springs Pool & Fitness Center.
STEWART M. GREEN

hot spring tour includes skiing at Monarch Mountain or Sunlight Mountain, or raft-ing on the Colorado, Roaring Fork, or upper Arkansas Rivers.

The Northern Rockies are home to three hot springs, all located in Steamboat Springs. Skiing, water sports on the Yampa River, and many miles of hiking in the Routt National Forest and Mount Zirkel Wilderness are close by.

Fifteen more hot springs in Southwest Colorado round out the state. Sprinkled from Creede to Pagosa Springs, Durango to Dolores, and Ridgway to Ouray, these hot springs may be a long drive for some, but if you're skiing in Telluride or Wolf Creek, ice-climbing in Ouray, or hiking in the San Juan Mountains, they're the perfect après ski, après climb, or après hike stop.

Two well-known hot springs are not included in this guide. Juniper Hot Springs, located west of Steamboat in Lay, is omitted, since the site was vandalized in 2017. As of the writing of this book, the pools have not been repaired. Hopefully, these outdoor pools will reopen at some point, as they present a good excuse to head northwest, perhaps to Dinosaur National Monument. Rico Hot Springs in Southwest Colorado is also omitted, as it has been signed as private property and so is off-limits.

Knowing a little bit about each area will make it easier for you to zero in on the best locations for your hot springs adventures. Then again, it may make the job even harder! Every one of the five hot springs regions of Colorado is spectacular in its own way, and if you have time, you'll want to visit them all.

Each of the forty-five hot springs chapters is laid out in a way that allows you to get the information you need up front to see if a hot spring is for you. From there you can choose to read on or skip to the next one.

The first section—the "planning section"—is basically a list of facts designed to give you an overview of the hot springs and answer your most important questions. This section tells you where the hot springs are and how to get to them, the accommodations available, the types of soaking and swimming options located at the site, and the restrictions that apply. If you want to know if you can camp at a hot spring, if bathing suits are required, and if they allow day-soakers—or if the hot springs are only reserved for overnight guests—you can find that information in the planning section. There's also an entry in this section with contact information, and you'll want to call ahead for rates, hours of operation, and reservations, if needed. All the commercial hot spring facilities in this book charge a fee for admittance, and the cost varies from minimal at some for a day pass to soak or swim, to hundreds of dollars at others for overnight stays in luxurious quarters. Of course, there's just about everything else in between, so you're sure to find something for your own budget. Some of the hot springs have a daily quota, and overnight accommodations such as lodges, cabins, yurts, tepees, tent sites, and RV spots can fill up quickly in the summer, so it's a good idea to make reservations well in advance, especially during the peak hot springs season from Memorial Day weekend through Labor Day. Also, some hot springs may close their entire facility for a few days to give the pools a thorough cleaning. Avoid surprises and possible disappointment by calling before you go.

Following the planning section is a short Overview of the site, followed by The Hot Springs section, which describes the soaking, swimming, and steaming options found there. Concrete swimming and soaking pools, hot soaking baths and jetted tubs, underground vapor caves and woodland ponds, and even creek-side natural pools are among the many types of hot springs found across the state.

The Site section comes next, with details about the rest of the hot springs facility, such as lodging and on-site athletic centers, spas, and salons.

Next, where information is available, some chapters include a Hot Springs History section, with a little information about the history of the site.

Lastly, some chapters end with an Area Highlights section with ideas for the best things to do in the area around the hot spring. These sections provide you with plenty of other ways to enjoy yourself on your Colorado hot springs tour.

Now that you know all about hot springs, and all about this book, it's time to dive into the hot springs chapters. Pour yourself a steamy cup of tea—or grab a cool bottle of mineral water—and get ready to immerse your mind, body, and spirit in hot springs splendor as you soak up the sights, sounds, and smells on your personal tour of Colorado's hot springs.

Facing page: A travertine waterfall borders the big soaking pool at Desert Reef Hot Spring.
STEWART M. GREEN

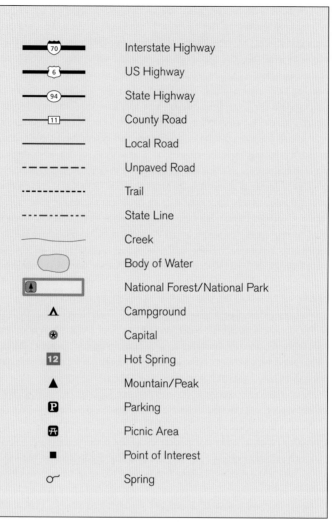

70	Interstate Highway
6	US Highway
94	State Highway
11	County Road
	Local Road
	Unpaved Road
	Trail
	State Line
	Creek
	Body of Water
	National Forest/National Park
▲	Campground
✪	Capital
12	Hot Spring
▲	Mountain/Peak
P	Parking
	Picnic Area
■	Point of Interest
⟀	Spring

FRONT RANGE COLORADO HOT SPRINGS

HOT SULPHUR SPRINGS, KREMMLING, IDAHO SPRINGS, ELDORADO SPRINGS, MANITOU SPRINGS, PENROSE, AND FLORENCE

Dozens of individual hot spring soaking and swimming pools, tubs, baths, geothermal caves, Jacuzzis, and one wild spring on the Colorado River are among the most accessible hot springs for people living in the populated cities of the Front Range. All are within a 2-hour drive from metropolitan Denver, and most are within a 2-hour drive from Colorado Springs.

The upper decks provide plenty of space to spread out and take in the sunshine at Eldorado Springs Pool. STEWART M. GREEN

1. HOT SULPHUR SPRINGS RESORT & SPA

Type: Family-oriented outdoor and indoor public and private swimming and soaking with quiet area, plus massage, spa services, and lodging.

Location: Hot Sulphur Springs, about 11 miles west of Granby.

When to visit: 7 days a week year-round for soaking. Swimming pool is open during the summer only.

Access: Year-round vehicle access on public roads. ADA access to swimming pool area and several lodge rooms.

Accommodations: 17-room motel lodge, 1 apartment, and 1 cabin.

Rules: Day-soakers welcome. Clothing is required in outdoor pools but optional in private baths. No smoking, no drugs, no alcohol, no glass, and no pets allowed. Food allowed in designated areas away from pools.

Services: Camping, gas, and limited dining and retail in Hot Sulphur Springs. Full services 11 miles east in Granby and 21 miles west in Kremmling.

Map & GPS: *DeLorme: Colorado Atlas & Gazetteer:* p. 28, E2; 40.074806 / -106.111710.

Contact: Hot Sulphur Springs Resort & Spa, 5609 CR 20, Hot Sulphur Springs, CO 80451; (970) 725-3306 or (800) 510-6235; http://hotsulphur springs.com. Call or visit website for rates, reservations, and hours of operation.

How to get there: From Denver, take I-70 West for about 29 miles, then take exit 232 to US 40 North for 56 miles to Hot Sulphur Springs. Turn right onto Park Street, left onto Spring Road, and left onto CR 20 to Hot Sulphur Springs.

OVERVIEW

Nestled along the Colorado River east of Kremmling, Hot Sulphur Springs Resort & Spa is pure nirvana for the hot springs connoisseur. Soaking pools built into tiered decking on a hillside and connected by a raised boardwalk welcome the casual or serious soaker. The staggered design, low fencing, Plexiglas dividers, and bench seating offer a semblance of privacy between pools without detracting from the open-air splendor and mountain views. The resort's location—about half an hour southwest of the western entrance to Rocky Mountain National Park—is surprisingly peaceful. Aside from the occasional train passing on the railway beyond the river, the only sound you may hear is your own breath as you sink into a soothing tub of hot mineral water and exhale your worries away.

The Hot Springs

Hot Sulphur Springs Resort & Spa boasts twenty-one soaking pools plus a swimming pool. In addition to the nineteen outdoor soaking pools—each one signed with a descriptive name and the water's temperature range—two private indoor baths with skylights, Sun Bath and Star Bath, are available for rent by the hour. Two additional private indoor baths are reserved for spa patrons.

The outdoor swimming pool ranges from 3 to 9 feet in depth and features a kiddie slide, plenty of decking, lounge chairs for sunning, and canopies for shade. This is the only pool that does not contain hot spring water, and it is only open during the summer.

There are quiet areas and places for play at Hot Sulphur Springs Resort & Spa, located about half an hour's drive from the western entrance to Rocky Mountain National Park.
PHOTOS BY STEWART M. GREEN

The soaking pools are open year-round. Four pools on the lower deck are kid-friendly and welcome water play, while pools on the upper decks are in a "quiet area" reserved for ages 12 and up. Some of the pools are in shaded, semi-enclosed areas, but most are in full sunlight.

Seven natural hot springs flow in Hot Sulphur Springs, and if you venture up the hillside, you'll find a sign marking one of them. Steaming mineral water rises from the depths at 104° to 126° and 5,000 gallons per hour. More than 200,000 gallons of water flow through the soaking pools at Hot Sulphur Springs daily, none of it is filtered or recirculated, and no chemicals are added.

The Site

A seventeen-room lodge accommodates overnight guests at Hot Sulphur Springs Resort & Spa. Cooking, smoking, alcohol, and pets are not allowed, and there are no televisions, so bring a good book and consider an appointment at the spa for a massage or other treatment. There's an apartment and a cabin for rent on-site as well, and the apartment includes 24-hour access to the pools. Like most hot springs, the Hot Sulphur Springs Resort & Spa does not allow food or beverages near the pools, but there is a picnic area, so bring a cooler of sandwiches, snacks, and drinks for your midday or evening break.

Hot Springs History

Ute Indians enjoyed Hot Sulphur Springs for many years before William Byers discovered the site in 1840 and, shortly after, took legal ownership. Byers was on the first recorded ascent of popular Colorado fourteener Longs Peak, and the scenic drive from Hot Sulphur Springs to Kremmling passes through his namesake, 8-mile-long Byers Canyon. The hot springs resort was kept in continuous operation for a century and a half until its temporary closure and renovation. In 1997, nearly 1,000 people attended the grand reopening, where the guest of honor, a Ute Indian spiritual leader, blessed the waters at Hot Sulphur Springs.

Area Highlights

Hot Sulphur Springs, the county seat of Grand County, comes alive for three days in June with a carnival, contests, live music, food, fireworks, and a parade at Hot Sulphur Days. Check www.hotsulphurdays.com for schedule.

Camping, hiking, mountain biking, wildlife viewing, and even a disc golf course are located next door to the hot springs at Pioneer Park State Wildlife Area. Fourteen first-come, first-served RV and tent camping sites with campfire areas and picnic tables make this a budget-friendly choice.

Start your day in Hot Sulphur Springs with a visit to the Pioneer Village Museum, then take a scenic drive west through Byers Canyon. For a longer drive, head 25 miles northeast to the town of Grand Lake, home to the largest and deepest natural lake in the state and the western gateway to Rocky Mountain National Park.

Whenever you visit Hot Sulphur Springs Resort & Spa, you'll find plenty to do in grand and wild Grand County.

2. RADIUM HOT SPRINGS

Type: Wild outdoor public soaking, plus primitive campground camping.

Location: Trailhead is located at O. C. Mugrage Campground, Radium State Wildlife Area, Sheephorn Unit, about 18 miles southwest of Kremmling. The hike to the hot springs is about 1.5 miles round-trip on BLM land along the Colorado River.

When to visit: Year-round, depending on access, but late spring to early winter is best. Spring runoff into the Colorado River can overrun the hot springs, and winter snow can make the scramble down to the hot springs slick and dangerous.

Access: Year-round access to the trailhead, but the hike up and scramble down to the hot spring may be affected by weather. No ADA access.

Accommodations: Primitive tent camping at the trailhead at O. C. Mugrage Campground. Additional tent camping at nearby Radium Recreation Site. Nearest motels are 18 miles northeast in Kremmling.

Rules: Clothing is recommended. Even though this is a wild spring, rafters and kayakers frequent the area and you will likely have an audience. Colorado State Wildlife Area regulations (http://cpw.state.co.us/aboutus/Pages/RulesRegs.aspx) apply at the trailhead, and BLM regulations (www.blm.gov/about/laws-and-regulations) apply on the trail and at the hot springs.

Services: Trailhead pit toilet. Full services are located 18 miles from the trailhead in Kremmling.

Maps & GPS: *DeLorme: Colorado Atlas & Gazetteer:* p. 28, E2; *National Geographic Trails Illustrated #120*, State Bridge, Burns; Radium Quadrangle. Trailhead 39.951350 / -106.542417; hot springs 39.959892 / -106.540715.

Contact: Colorado Parks & Wildlife (CPW), Radium State Wildlife Area, Hot Sulphur Springs Area CPW Office, (970) 725-6200, http://cpw.state.co.us; Bureau of Land Management, Kremmling Field Office, (970) 724-3000, www.blm.gov.

How to get there: From Denver, take I-70 West for about 55 miles, then take exit 205 to CO 9 North and go 35 miles. Turn left onto CR 1/Trough Road. Drive the dirt road for 14.5 miles, turn right onto CR 11, and continue 1.4 miles to O. C. Mugrage Campround, on the left. Park in the big dirt lot just past the toilet. The trail to Radium Hot Springs is in view across the road, on the hillside.

OVERVIEW

Radium Hot Springs is the closest wild spring to the Denver area and popular year-round. If you have a 4WD with high clearance, you can drive past the campground and get closer to the hot springs to shorten the hike, or float right up to it on a raft. Most soakers reach Radium Hot Springs on foot, and an easy trail and short scramble take you right to it.

The Hot Springs

Like all undeveloped hot springs, the size, temperature, and overall condition of Radium Hot Springs vary with the seasons and precipitation, snowmelt, and overflow

Above: Rafters are common, and so clothing is recommended at Radium Hot Springs. SUSAN JOY PAUL

Below: Most soakers reach Radium Hot Springs on foot via an easy trail and short scramble down to the riverbank. STEWART M. GREEN

from the adjacent river. In the spring of 2017, the pool was roughly 20 feet in diameter, 2 feet deep, and 90° at the source, which is located close to the riverbank, cooling to about 80° around the perimeter.

The Site

The hike to Radium Hot Springs begins at O. C. Mugrage Campground, located along Sheephorn Creek, on State Wildlife Area property. This is a primitive site, but there's a pit toilet and fire rings, and dispersed tent camping is free.

To reach the hot springs, cross CR 11 and hike north, up the steep trail, which levels out at 0.16 mile. At 0.44 mile, veer northeast on the trail, paralleling the river, and at 0.70 mile, head

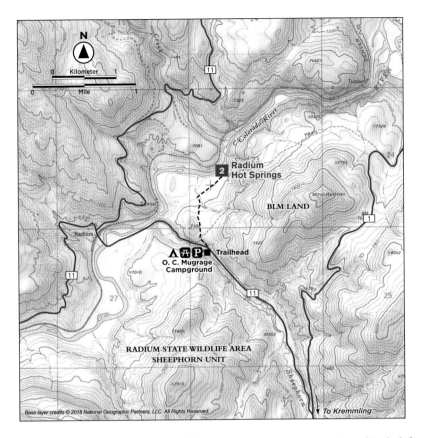

north toward the river. Peer over the cliff to find the hot springs below, located to the left of an outcropping that's popular with cliff divers. Descend the steep, rocky trail about 40 feet. The pool is surrounded by rocks to keep the warm spring water in and cool river out.

If you camp at Mugrage, follow the posted rules, and if you have a campfire, observe fire restrictions and never leave a fire unattended. Use only dead wood and existing fire rings to avoid additional impact to the land, extinguish campfires completely before your departure, and ensure the ashes are cold. Camp at least 100 feet from water sources, and dispose of all wash water at least 200 feet from the river and hot springs. Use the pit toilet, or bury human waste far from the river and carry out everything else, including toilet paper and other personal products.

As with all wild springs, follow Leave No Trace principles (https://lnt.org) to ensure a pristine environment for your next visit and for other visitors to the area.

Area Highlights
If you prefer to float to the hot springs, head to nearby Kremmling and rent a kayak, tube, or raft, or book a guided trip down the Colorado River. For more adventures, Wolford Mountain Recreation Area is located 8 miles north of Kremmling. Enjoy hiking, wildlife viewing, mountain biking, and camping on BLM land.

3. INDIAN HOT SPRINGS

Type: Family-oriented, resort-style outdoor and indoor public and private swimming, soaking, Jacuzzis, mud bath, and geothermal cave baths, plus massage and spa services and lodging.

Location: Idaho Springs, about 32 miles west of Denver and 13 miles south of Black Hawk.

When to visit: 7 days a week year-round. Call ahead or check website for dates of occasional pool closures.

Access: Year-round vehicle access on public roads. ADA access to pool. Call for details.

Accommodations: 20-room historic resort, 28-room modern lodge, 20-room inn, and 4 cabins.

Rules: Day-soakers welcome. Clothing is required in community pool and Club Mud, but optional in private baths, private Jacuzzis, and gender-specific geothermal baths. No smoking, no drugs, no alcohol, no glass, and no pets allowed. Food allowed in designated areas away from pools.

Services: Full services in Idaho Springs.

Map & GPS: *DeLorme: Colorado Atlas & Gazetteer*: p. 39, C7; 39.739283 / -105.512626.

Contact: Indian Hot Springs, 302 Soda Creek Rd., PO Box 1990, Idaho Springs, CO 80452; (303) 989-6666; www.indianhotsprings.com. Call or visit website for rates, discounts, reservations, and hours of operation.

How to get there: From Denver, take I-70 West for 21.3 miles, then take exit 240 and drive 0.1 mile. Turn right onto 13th Avenue, right on Miner Street, and right on Soda Creek Road to Indian Hot Springs, on the left.

OVERVIEW

Located between Denver and recreation destinations to the west, Indian Hot Springs is an easy temptation for weekend warriors returning to the big city. Don't wait for that next big ski trip, though: at less than an hour's drive from the metro area, Indian Hot Springs makes a great weekend or midweek getaway.

The Hot Springs

With more than 60,000 gallons of hot spring water flowing through twenty-three pools at one hundred gallons per minute daily, you're sure to find a soak that suits you at Indian Hot Springs. The big communal swimming pool sits under a translucent dome and is surrounded by tropical plants and trees. This pool is fed by 115° mineral water, which cools to between 90° and 100°, depending on the season. A small pool partitioned within the larger pool is somewhat hotter. The effect is much like soaking in the middle of a lush, green rain forest, and this is a great choice for families.

On the other side of the building, adults can enjoy quiet, clothing-optional baths carved into underground vapor caves. The geothermal baths are piping hot, with water emerging at 126° and cooling to a sultry 104° to 112°. There are four baths on the women's side and three baths on the men's side.

Top: The translucent dome offers a greenhouse-like setting for a soak at Indian Hot Springs.
Bottom: Private hot spring Jacuzzis bubble with the touch of a button at Indian Hot Springs.
PHOTOS BY STEWART M. GREEN

Indian Hot Springs has indoor and outdoor private soaking. Eleven individual indoor soaking tubs, filled with hot spring water at about 104° to 106°, may be rented by the hour. The tiled tubs are about 8 feet long, 6 feet wide, and 4 feet deep, and each private bath area also houses a shower and bench seating. If you prefer your soak out of doors, four Jacuzzi tubs are available, filled with steamy 104° to 109° hot spring water. Push-button electric jets provide a relaxing hydromassage in the open air. Each Jacuzzi is surrounded on three sides by a 6-foot-high fence, with one side open to the hillside for a woodsy feel (and occasional wildlife viewing), and there's a shower and seating in each compartment.

Newly remodeled Club Mud features a large earthen bowl filled with mineral-rich clay. Slather yourself in the slippery mixture, and relax on a lounge chair while the mud dries to a skin-tightening body mask. After about 45 minutes, wash away the clay and impurities drawn from your pores in a warm shower.

The Site

Along with all the hot springs choices, Indian Hot Springs has sundecks, an event space, a gift shop, and an assortment of historic and modern overnight accommodations. Full spa and massage services are available, too, so your only challenge may be trying to make up your mind as to which rooms, massages, treatments, and soaks to choose.

Hot Springs History

Soda Creek once marked the neutral ground between the Ute and Arapaho Indians, and the development at Indian Hot Springs dates back to the middle of the nineteenth century. In 1863, Dr. E. M. Cummings bought the property and began charging for hot soaks, and in 1866 the "Hot Water Mine" was sold to Harrison Montague, who replaced the existing wooden structure with a stone "Ocean Bath House." Other owners added or subtracted bits of history from Indian Hot Springs' structure, and today it stands as a sprawling montage of old and new.

Area Highlights

While you're in the area, tour the Phoenix Mine or Argo Mine, ride the Georgetown Loop Railroad, or drive the Mount Evans Scenic Byway, the highest paved road in North America. If you have transportation, drive to nearby Black Hawk, home to more gambling casinos than any other town in the state. Buses, taxis, and services like Uber do not drive from Idaho Springs to Black Hawk, so plan ahead. Whatever mode of transportation you choose, you'll likely meet up with wildlife at some point. Bighorn sheep, elk, mule deer, mountain goats, black bears, and mountain lions all call Clear Creek County home. Keep a safe distance and enjoy the experience.

From skiing at Loveland Ski Area, snowboarding at Echo Mountain, and snow-shoeing on miles of trails, to rock climbing at Clear Creek Canyon, whitewater rafting on Clear Creek, and hiking and biking throughout the county, there's plenty to do in Clear Creek County. Imagine how good that soak back at Indian Hot Springs will feel after a day on the slopes, crags, river, or trail.

4. **ELDORADO SPRINGS POOL**

Type: Family-oriented outdoor public swimming and soaking, plus event space.

Location: Eldorado Springs, about 30 miles northwest of Denver and 9 miles south of Boulder.

When to visit: 7 days a week from Memorial Day weekend through Labor Day.

Access: Year-round vehicle access on private road. Call ahead for ADA access details.

Accommodations: None on-site, but tent camping, RV parks, and motels are located 11 miles east in Louisville and 17 miles south in Golden.

Rules: Day-soaker facility. Clothing is required. No smoking, no drugs, no alcohol, no glass, and no pets allowed.

Services: No services in Eldorado Springs, but full services are available in Boulder and Louisville.

Map & GPS: *DeLorme: Colorado Atlas & Gazetteer:* p. 40, A1; 39.932352 / -105.279053.

Contact: Eldorado Springs Swimming Pool, 294 Artesian Dr., Eldorado Springs, CO 80025; (303) 604-3000; www.eldoradosprings.com/swimming-pool. Call or visit website for rates and hours of operation.

How to get there: From Denver, take I-25 North to exit 217A and get onto US 36 West. Continue 14.1 miles and take the McCaslin Boulevard exit. Turn left onto McCaslin Boulevard and then right onto CO 170/Marshall Road. Drive 3.8 miles and turn left onto CO 170/Eldorado Springs Drive. Continue on the dirt road for about 3 miles, bearing left at the fork. Park in the lot on the left side of the road and cross the road to Eldorado Hot Springs.

OVERVIEW

Once known as "Coney Island West," the Eldorado Springs Pool is a slice of pure old-fashioned Americana, just a short drive from the Denver metro area but worlds away from the daily grind of big-city life. Tucked into Eldorado Canyon and protected on all sides by high cliffs, shade trees, and South Boulder Creek, it's a warm, sunny spot with a big pool of warm spring water and enough features to make it fun, affordable, and a great way to spend an afternoon.

This is the oldest swimming pool in the state, and they've kept much of the original charm. It's also very neat, clean, and well maintained—the perfect spot to bring your family for the day. They'll have a good time in the crystal-clear waters while you enjoy the summer breezes. The pool is only open from Memorial Day weekend through Labor Day, so put it on your calendar. This is vintage swimming at its best.

The Hot Springs

Warm 76° spring water from an on-site artesian spring fills the Eldorado Springs Pool. The water is constantly replenished, lightly chlorinated, and maintained at 78° to 80°—a wonderful respite from the summer swelter after a day of hiking in nearby Eldorado Canyon State Park. The pool is a big 120 feet long by 40 feet wide, and there's

After a hike or a climb in Eldorado Canyon, head to the Eldorado Springs Pool. Enjoy a soak, a dip, or a dive. The big old-fashioned slide is a favorite. PHOTOS BY STEWART M. GREEN

a classic metal slide at the shallow end and a diving board at the deep end. Lifeguards are on duty at all times. Bring your own towel, pool toys, and lounge chairs.

The Site

The Eldorado Springs Pool is bordered by sandstone cliffs, a bubbling creek, and shady elm, cottonwood, box elder, and ash trees. You can eat at the snack bar or enjoy your own picnic lunch on a creekside picnic table. Live jazz music is featured occasionally during the summer, so don't be surprised if your afternoon meal, soak, or swim is accompanied by the sounds of sweet strings and gentle brass.

The natural spring here also supplies the Eldorado Natural Spring Water bottling company, and there's a tap on-site, so bring a little money and some containers; for a small fee, you can stay hydrated all day long and take some home with you too.

Hot Springs History

The first pool was built here in 1905, and in 1908, the New Eldorado Hotel opened, attracting wealthy patrons and celebrities. During the 1970s, when interest in the canyon grew as a potential quarry, the State of Colorado purchased 272 acres, and the land was established as Eldorado Canyon State Park.

In 1983, the current owners of the Eldorado Springs Pool, Doug Larson and Jeremy Martin (along with former co-owner Kevin Sipple), purchased the pool, 28 acres of land, water rights, and numerous structures, and they restored the historic swimming pool. Doug Larson's wife, Kathy, managed the pool for many years until their daughter, Erica Larson, took over in 2015. Meanwhile, Doug Larson and Jeremy Martin grew their water bottling company, Eldorado Artesian Springs Inc., into a $15-million-a-year business. You can purchase Eldorado Natural Spring Water at your local grocer, but if you want to bathe in it, you'll have to come up to Eldorado Springs and take a dip in the big pool.

Area Highlights

The town of Eldorado Springs is a lovely place to visit, but you'll want to plan ahead. Other than the snack bar at the pool, you're on your own for food, so pack a lunch.

Eldorado Canyon came to national attention in 1907 when tightrope walker Ivy Baldwin crossed a 635-foot-wide section of the canyon on a thin cable, over 582 feet of air—without a net! In 2016, slackliner Taylor VanAllen made the first crossing on a highline. From the 1950s to the 1970s, rock-climbing pioneers Layton Kor and Jim Erickson made their mark in the canyon, putting up first ascents on the Bastille, Wind Tower, and Redgarden Wall.

Today, anyone can enjoy the crags here without the mad skills and derring-do of Baldwin, Kor, Erickson, or VanAllen, as the canyon attracts hordes of rock climbers. For low-angle fun, pick up a hiking trail map at the Eldorado Canyon State Park Visitor Center. Just remember, from Memorial Day weekend to Labor Day, after a long day on the cliffs or the trails, by the creek, or on the crags, there's a big pool of fresh spring water waiting for you at the Eldorado Springs Pool.

5. SUNWATER SPA

Type: Cozy, quiet outdoor and indoor public and private soaking, plus massage and spa services and nearby lodging.

Location: Manitou Springs, about 6 miles northwest of Colorado Springs.

When to visit: 7 days a week year-round. Reservations are highly recommended for spa services.

Access: Year-round vehicle access on public roads. Call ahead for ADA access details.

Accommodations: None on-site, but associated SunMountain Center bed-and-breakfast/retreat is located 0.5 mile away, and RV parks and motels are located in Manitou Springs.

Rules: Day-soaker facility. Clothing is required. No smoking, no drugs, no alcohol, no glass, and no pets allowed. No tours.

Services: Full services in Manitou Springs.

Map & GPS: *DeLorme: Colorado Atlas & Gazetteer:* p. 62, B4; 38.858570 / -104.910957.

Contact: SunWater Spa, 514 El Paso Blvd., Manitou Springs, CO 80829; (719) 695-7007; www.sunwellness.net. Call or visit website for rates, reservations, and hours of operation.

How to get there: From Colorado Springs, take Colorado Avenue west to Manitou Avenue. Drive 1.5 miles and turn right onto Old Mans Trail, then left onto El Paso Boulevard.

OVERVIEW

Colorado's newest hot spring is a meditative experience fitting the town of Manitou Springs. SunWater Spa and nearby SunMountain Center embody a culture of wellness, reflected in soaking, therapies, massage, yoga, food, farming, lodging, and retreats. The calm, quiet atmosphere, subdued lighting, gentle sounds, and natural scents combine to lift your spirits and lighten your being.

The Hot Springs

The water at SunWater Spa isn't technically hot springs water, but mineral water from 7 Minute Spring, a cold spring located across the street beneath a gazebo. The water is piped in and heated (primarily with solar panels) in eight large cedar soaking tubs to a temperature of 100° to 104°. Seven of the tubs are public and one is private, but all are filled with a steamy cedar "tea" of minerals drawn from the earth and oils from the cedar tubs. The private tub, located outside but out of view of other soakers, seats four and is available for rent by the hour.

The public cedar tubs are located on the deck, with views of Pikes Peak to the west and the city of Manitou Springs, below. An indoor therapy pool and hot and cold plunges are filled with municipal water and saline is added. Finally, the Zen Meditation Stream combines basalt rocks with mineral water for a refreshing walk and gentle acupressure to soothe your soles.

Facing page, top: An indoor therapy pool and hot and cold plunges are filled with municipal water to which saline is added. Bottom left: The private tub at SunWater Spa seats four and is available for rent by the hour. Bottom right: The pitter patter of a mineral spring waterfall greets visitors to SunWater Spa. PHOTOS BY STEWART M. GREEN

SunWater Spa and nearby SunMountain Center embody a culture of wellness, reflected in soaking, therapies, massage, yoga, food, farming, lodging, and retreats. COURTESY SUNWATER SPA

The Site

Soaking is a small part of the offerings at SunWater Spa, and most people come here for the array of treatments and therapies. Watsu, facials, scrubs, wraps, muds, and massage are offered, often in combination with soaking. If you like the services, you can purchase many of the products here too. SunWater Spa also has a wellness facility and a full calendar of events, including yoga, tai chi, dance, meditation, and classes that incorporate soaking, like aqua yoga. Workshops are also offered regularly.

SunMountain is the lodging and retreat part of SunWellness, and individual rooms are offered bed-and-breakfast style, or you can reserve space for your group as a retreat.

Hot Springs History

Eight carbonated mineral springs—Cheyenne, Iron Geyser, Navajo, 7 Minute, Shoshone, Wheeler, Stratton, and Twin—spring from the Manitou Springs artesian aquifer. Small structures and fountains provide visitors with a taste of the waters, but it wasn't until 2015 that someone decided to harness the water for soaking. Kat Tudor and Don Goede renovated a hundred-year-old home and built a 6,000 square foot, three-level structure to house the soaking tubs and services.

Area Highlights

Two of southern Colorado's most popular hikes begin in Manitou Springs: Barr Trail leads to Barr Camp and, eventually, all the way to the summit of Pikes Peak. Round-trip, this is a 26-mile hike to 14,115 feet, so before you go, research the route and plan to start very early. Alternatively, the Pikes Peak Cog Railway is also located in town, or you can head east on US 24 and drive Pikes Peak Highway to the top of the mountain.

Next to Barr Trailhead is the Manitou Incline, an old railroad track that climbs steeply—more than 2,000 feet in less than a mile—up the hillside. From the top, hikers descend Barr Trail.

Manitou Springs is an artsy town that attracts a lot of tourists, so there are plenty of shops and restaurants, plus a fun and lively penny arcade. Live it up out there—you'll find plenty of peace and quiet back at SunWater Spa.

6. DAKOTA HOT SPRINGS

Type: Rustic, quiet outdoor public swimming and soaking, plus camping.

Location: Penrose, about 36 miles southwest of Colorado Springs and 10 miles east of Cañon City.

When to visit: 7 days a week year-round.

Access: Year-round vehicle access on public roads. ADA access to sun-decks, canopies, and restroom with shower and benches.

Accommodations: Tent and RV camping. No hookups, but the bathhouse is available for use by overnight guests. Motels are located 7 miles southwest in Florence, and camping and RV parks are located 8 miles north in Penrose.

Rules: Day-soakers welcome. Clothing is optional except on Tuesday, when swimsuits are required. Service pets allowed. No glass, cameras, cell phones, or any devices with a camera in them.

Services: Limited services in Florence and Penrose; full services 10 miles west in Cañon City.

Map & GPS: *DeLorme: Colorado Atlas & Gazetteer:* p. 72, A2; 38.418338 / -105.056473.

Contact: Dakota Hot Springs, 1 Malibu Blvd., Penrose, CO 81240; (719) 372-9250; www.dakotahotsprings.com. Call or visit website for rates and hours of operation.

How to get there: From Colorado Springs, take CO 115 South for 35 miles and turn left onto Malibu Boulevard. Continue 0.4 mile to Dakota Hot Springs.

OVERVIEW

Dakota Hot Springs, formerly known as "The Well," is an outdoor hot spring pool located in the Arkansas Valley, surprisingly close to a highway yet offering a comfortably private, lively place to take in the waters, sans suit or otherwise. Easy access, a laid-back atmosphere, and a "good clean fun" culture that's nurtured and protected by the management—coupled with a sunny, moderate climate—make this a popular year-round spot for sun and spring worshipers alike.

The Hot Springs

There's one big outdoor pool at Dakota Hot Springs for soaking, swimming, and water play. An artesian well, flowing at 300 gallons per minute, fills a 6-foot-wide tub at the center of the pool with 108° water, making for a steamy soak. The water spills from the tub into the 70-foot-wide, free-form concrete pool that's maintained at 95° to 98° in summer months, 100° to 108° in winter. The pool's depth ranges from 3 to 5 feet deep, and there's a volleyball net set up on one end. The water is slightly carbonated and rich in mineral salts, soda, and calcium; because it contains only trace amounts of sulfur compounds, there is no sulfurous odor.

Water flows freely into and back out of the pool, there is no recirculation, and no chlorine is added. A communal lounging area keeps winter chills at bay with a wood-stove at its center, and there's plenty of surrounding glass to guard the most scantily protected loungers from wayward breezes.

Top: Concrete and wooden decks, a cabana, and canopies offer year-round sun and shade to soakers and sunbathers at Dakota Hot Springs. Bottom: Dakota Hot Springs is one of only a few hot springs that feature a volleyball net. PHOTOS BY SUSAN JOY PAUL

The Site

Dakota Hot Springs is located in Colorado's "banana belt," an area that averages 56° and 350 days of sunshine annually, making for a pleasant atmosphere even in winter months. Alongside the pool are a bathhouse, concrete and wooden decks, a cabana, and shade canopies. Snacks, bottled water, and soft drinks are available for purchase, and outside food and beverages are allowed, but leave glass bottles at home. A barbecue grill and microwave are available for your use. Dakota Hot Springs has a loyal clientele, and if you decide to join their ranks, expect to be invited to a potluck or other poolside social event.

Hot Springs History

Dakota Hot Springs is fed by an artesian well that was drilled, and then abandoned, by the Continental Oil Company in 1924, when water—instead of oil—was discovered at 2,000 feet. That's lucky for those in the southern Front Range, who are merely a hop, skip, and a plunge from a friendly and welcoming facility that attracts a dedicated crowd year-round.

Area Highlights

Hot springs enthusiasts with an active zeal will appreciate Dakota Hot Springs' proximity to Cañon City, where opportunities for hiking, biking, rock climbing, kayaking, and whitewater rafting abound. Or head north on CO 115 to Colorado Springs, where even more rock and trails await you. Guides may be found for just about any activity in both Cañon City and Colorado Springs, and many will accept you on a walk-in basis.

For self-guided tours, pick up a guidebook for Shelf Road in Cañon City or Garden of the Gods, Red Rock Canyon Open Space, and North Cheyenne Canyon in the Pikes Peak region. There are thrilling mountain drives too. Pikes Peak Highway will take you to the 14,115-foot summit of "America's mountain," Pikes Peak, or enjoy leisurely drives along scenic Gold Camp Road and Rampart Range Road. Be sure to visit Garden of the Gods, which has paved and dirt trails, plus some of the finest sandstone towers you will ever see in a free and open state park. Whatever you do, you'll surely appreciate the hustle and bustle of the big city even more, knowing that you can always relax back at Dakota Hot Springs.

Dakota Hot Springs is located in Colorado's "banana belt," an area that averages 56° and 350 days of sunshine annually. SUSAN JOY PAUL

7. **DESERT REEF HOT SPRING**

Type: Rustic, quiet outdoor public swimming and soaking.

Location: Florence, about 40 miles southwest of Colorado Springs and 15 miles southeast of Cañon City.

When to visit: Wednesday through Sunday year-round. Closed Monday for cleaning and Tuesday for events, but call ahead or check website for updates.

Access: Year-round vehicle access on public road, but not accessible by large motor homes. ADA access to pool area.

Accommodations: None on-site, but motels are located 5 miles west in Florence, and tent camping, RV parks, and motels are located 14 miles northwest in Cañon City.

Rules: Day-soaker facility. Must present ID at first visit. Clothing is optional Wednesday, Saturday, and Sunday; swimsuits are required on Thursday and Friday. No pets, radios, cameras, TVs, cell phones, pagers, computers, PDAs, or other communication or recording devices. No drugs or controlled substances allowed on the premises. No glass near the pool area.

Services: Limited services in Florence and Penrose; full services in Cañon City.

Map & GPS: *DeLorme: Colorado Atlas & Gazetteer:* p. 72, B3; 38.368617 / -105.049354.

Contact: Desert Reef Hot Spring, 1194 CR 110, Florence, CO 81226; (719) 784-6134; www.desertreefhotspring .com. Call or visit website for rates and hours of operation.

How to get there: From Colorado Springs, take CO 115 South for 35 miles and turn left onto CO 120. Drive 1.1 miles and turn right onto CR 110. Continue another 1.5 miles, proceeding across a bridge, over a dip in the road, and through a gate to Desert Reef Hot Spring.

OVERVIEW

Tucked at the end of a winding road in Royal Gorge country, Desert Reef Hot Spring is a hidden gem, simple in its development and serene in its starkness. The hot spring makes use of an oasis-like setting to offer its clients a soothing and relaxing place to soak, float, or catch some rays, without worrying about tan lines. Desert Reef provides its guests with a unique sense of solitude with its secluded location that is set back 1.5 miles from the main road. The desert setting and unobstructed mountain views complete the experience.

The Hot Springs

Desert Reef Hot Spring includes a single, free-form concrete pool measuring 36 by 50 feet and brimming with 40,400 gallons of crystal-blue, calcium-rich, sulfur-free hot spring water. Sourced from an on-site artesian well, the water gushes from the earth at 130 gallons per minute and tumbles into the pool with a steady flow that's maintained at 94° to 96° in the summer and 100° to 102° in winter. The lovely aqua

Facing page, top left: The hula girls point the way to Desert Reef Hot Spring. Top right: A solo soaker soaks up the sunshine at Desert Reef Hot Spring. Bottom: Desert Reef Hot Spring has clothing-optional and clothing-required days. PHOTOS BY STEWART M. GREEN

Desert Reef Hot Spring attracts a loyal clientele. STEWART M. GREEN

tint is a result of natural travertine minerals, while the occasional waterfall is sculpted mainly of calcium deposited by water traveling from well to pool. No chlorine is added to the water.

The Site

Situated on 10 acres of peace and quiet in the Arkansas Valley, Desert Reef Hot Spring is protected by a privacy berm on one end and open to views of the Wet Mountains on the other. Concrete decks, a shady canopy, lounge chairs, picnic tables, and a barbecue grill surround the pool. No food is provided, so pack a lunch, snacks, and drinks. Beside the pool there's a greenhouse lounge where guests can use the refrigerator, microwave, and water cooler. The management at Desert Reef seeks to maintain a gender balance and requests that single men visiting the hot springs be accompanied by a female companion.

Hot Springs History

Like most other hot springs in this area of the state, Desert Reef benefited from early hit-or-miss Conoco Oil drilling that resulted in gushing waters rather than oil. A Florence oil exploration project in the 1940s discovered the hot springs, and the original well—dug more than 4,000 feet below the ground—was plugged at 1,096 feet, providing a manageable flow of 132° hot mineral water for the current artesian well.

Area Highlights

Spend some time in Florence, where you'll find shops, restaurants, and the Florence Pioneer Museum and Research Center. The Historic Rialto Theater is being renovated but continues to showcase dinner theater and other events.

Scenic drives are close by, like the 58-mile Wet Mountains Scenic Drive from Florence to Colorado City, with canyon views and rest stops at Bishop Castle and Lake Isabel. The Gold Belt Tour Scenic and Historic Byway—running from Florence to Florissant—encompasses 135 miles of delightfully scenic opportunities for historical and geographical enlightenment at places like Cripple Creek, the Royal Gorge, and Florissant Fossil Beds.

If you're short on time, enjoy the 3-mile paved road up Skyline Drive in Cañon City, offering views from the crest of an 800-foot Dakota hogback and littered with the preserved footprints of dinosaurs. You can even get out of the car for a closer look if you like! You may need a long soak back at Desert Reef Hot Spring after all this excitement.

SAN LUIS VALLEY COLORADO HOT SPRINGS

VILLA GROVE, HOOPER, MOSCA, AND ALAMOSA

Bound to the west by the San Juan Mountains and to the east by the Sangre de Cristo Range, Colorado's sunny San Luis Valley is known for sand dunes, UFO sightings, and hot mineral springs! Five commercial hot springs vary from naturist sanctuary to cozy soaking pools, family-friendly swimming pools, and even an alligator park. All are located within a 3- to 4-hour drive from Denver and Colorado Springs.

Enjoy mountain views at Sand Dunes Recreation in the San Luis Vallley. STEWART M. GREEN

8. VALLEY VIEW HOT SPRINGS AT ORIENT LAND TRUST

Type: Rustic, quiet outdoor public swimming and soaking, plus sauna, massage, camping, and lodging.

Location: Saguache County near Villa Grove, about 38 miles south of Salida.

When to visit: 7 days a week year-round EXCEPT December 1 through December 28, when the site is closed. Reservations HIGHLY recommended.

Access: Year-round vehicle access on public roads. Call ahead for ADA access details.

Accommodations: Tent camping; vehicle camping and a few sites have electricity but there are no full hook-ups and no dump station, and generators are not allowed; dormitory, private rooms, 5 cabins, 3 with kitchenettes; other kitchens are communal; all bathrooms facilities are shared and coed.

Rules: Day-soakers welcome, but nonmembers should call 24 hours ahead as preference is given to land-trust member donors, who can make advance reservations; there are capacity limits, and the facility is often booked. Clothing is optional, and nudity is predominant but not required. No cell service. Smoking allowed in your vehicle or in the Smoking Hut only. No glass containers allowed. Alcohol allowed in moderation, but intoxication is not. Pets welcome, but there are fees and a leash requirement, so call ahead. Quiet hours from 10 p.m. to 8 a.m., and no admittance between 10 p.m. and 9 a.m. (gates are locked). Pools are open 24 hours for overnight guests.

Services: Limited services in nearby Villa Grove, Saguache, and Moffat; full services 24 miles south in Crestone and 33 miles north in Poncha Springs.

Map & GPS: *DeLorme: Colorado Atlas & Gazetteer*: p. 70, C4; 38.192247 / -105.815227.

Contact: Valley View Hot Springs, 64393 CR GG, Moffat, CO 81143; (719) 256-4315; www.olt.org/vvhs. Call or visit website for rates, reservations, and hours of operation.

How to get there: From Salida, take US 50 West for 3.9 miles and turn left onto US 285 South. Drive 26.3 miles and turn left onto CO 17. Immediately bear left onto CR GG. Continue 7.3 miles to Valley View Hot Springs.

OVERVIEW

Nestled on the eastern edge of Saguache County, at the base of the Sangre de Cristo Mountains, Valley View Hot Springs is a secluded open-air retreat and part of the Orient Land Trust, a nonprofit entity dedicated to the preservation of natural resources within its more than 2,200 acres. In a setting worthy of woodland nymphs, sprites, and magical creatures, the hot springs at Valley View not only feed the pools and ponds but also fuel the hydroelectric system that provides all the electricity to the facility and land trust. In keeping with the mind-set of treading lightly on the lands, waters, and wildlife, Valley View operates entirely "off the grid."

The swimming pool at Valley View is 80 feet long, 3 to 9 feet deep, and 87° to 92°, with concrete decks for sunning, a bathhouse for changing, and a 160° sauna. STEWART M. GREEN

The Hot Springs

Eleven soaking and swimming options are fed by natural, non-chlorinated, non-sulfurous, hot spring mineral water that's 100° at the source and 88° to 108° in the pools and ponds.

The swimming pool is 75 feet long, 3 to 8 feet deep, and 87° to 92°, with concrete decks for sunning, a bathhouse, and a 160° sauna with an 88° fresh dip pool inside. The nearby Baby Pool is 96° to 97°. The Apple Tree Pools, constructed in 2013, are the hottest pools at 103° to 108° and filled with hydroelectrically heated fresh water that isn't treated or recirculated. A short hike takes you to six natural ponds of varying temperatures, depending on the season and weather. The Soaking Pond is 96° to 98°; the Waterfall Pond is 95° to 98°; the Meadow Pond is 94° to 98°; and three connecting ponds make up the Top Pond, with temperatures ranging from 70° to 100°. Each has its own shape, size, and personality, and provides superb mountain vistas. The pools and ponds at Valley View Hot Springs are open to overnight guests 24 hours a day. No chlorine is added to any of the pools, ponds, or sauna.

The Site

The three large cabins have kitchenettes, while guests of the smaller two cabins share a communal kitchen with the Oak House, a lodge with shared sleeping areas and bunk beds. The Sunset House lodge has private bedrooms and a shared kitchen. Spruce Lodge has two private bedrooms and a shared kitchen and full bath. No food is provided, so pack what you need. All accommodations at Valley View have shared, coed bathrooms. There are lots of porches wrapped around the properties, and a large

Nestled on the eastern edge of Saguache County, at the base of the Sangre de Cristo Mountains, Valley View Hot Springs is a secluded open-air retreat and part of the Orient Land Trust. SCOTT RAPPOLD–COURTESY VALLEY VIEW

picnic pavilion provides campers with an outdoor kitchen. The current method for obtaining advance reservations is tied to donations to the land trust, and a phone call to the resort will answer your questions about how to best ensure accommodations for your visit. Valley View has daily quotas, admitting just 35 day-soakers and 105 overnight guests daily, so call before you go.

The Orient Mine closed many years ago and is now inhabited by the largest bat colony in Colorado. A 4-mile round-trip hike takes you to the site, where you can view their spectacular outflight. Valley View also offers geology tours, astronomy tours, sustainable energy hydro tours, and a variety of educational programs. Contact Valley View or check their website for details.

Hot Springs History

Archaeological finds at Valley View—such as pottery shards and arrowheads—remind us that Ute Indians once thrived in this area. Entrepreneur John Everson developed the site with buildings catering to the mining community. The land and waters at Valley View eventually came into the ownership of Neil and Terry Seitz, who formed the land trust in 2001 and donated the hot springs and surrounding lands to the trust in 2009.

Area Highlights

From the San Luis Valley to Great Sand Dunes National Park and the Sangre de Cristo Mountains, Saguache County runs the gamut from mild to wild outdoor adventures. There's rock climbing at Penitente Canyon, sand-sledding at the sand dunes, and hiking at South Crestone Lake and Willow Lake. The county seat, Saguache, is about 24 miles west of Valley View on US 285.

If you visit in the summer, enjoy the annual Saguache Hollyhock Festival, Saguache Arts Festival, and Inter-Tribal Pow-Wow Celebration, and in September there's the Saguache Fall Festival & Quilt Show. Or head southeast to Crestone, home to a Buddhist stupa, a Zen center, and other interreligious learning centers and retreats. Crestone celebrates a WinterFest in December, a good opportunity to purchase unique gifts from the local artists and artisans.

Be sure to gas up the car and pick up some groceries before heading back to Valley View at Orient Land Trust, where you can enjoy an evening soak and think about the next day's plan during your visit to Colorado's beautiful San Luis Valley.

The pools and ponds at Valley View Hot Springs are open to overnight guests 24 hours a day.
CYNTHIA NIELSEN–COURTESY VALLEY VIEW

9. JOYFUL JOURNEY HOT SPRINGS SPA

Type: Cozy, quiet outdoor and indoor public and private soaking and spa services, plus lodging.

Location: Saguache County near Villa Grove, about 30 miles south of Salida.

When to visit: 7 days a week year-round.

Access: Year-round vehicle access on public roads. Call ahead for ADA access details.

Accommodations: 11-room lodge, 7 yurts (2 pet-friendly), and 3 tepees (seasonally). Tent camping and RV hookups but no dump station.

Rules: Day-soakers welcome. Clothing is required in outdoor pools and optional in private indoor baths. Smoking allowed in the cannabis-friendly pavilion only. Pets allowed with paid fee and must be on leashes or in the pet pen.

Services: Limited services in nearby Villa Grove and Moffat; full services 15 miles west in Saguache and 25 miles south in Crestone.

Map & GPS: *DeLorme: Colorado Atlas & Gazetteer:* p. 70, D3; 38.168633 / -105.924838.

Contact: Joyful Journey Hot Springs Spa, 28640 CR 58EE, Moffat, CO 81143; (719) 256-4328; http://joyful journeyhotsprings.com. Call or visit website for rates, reservations, and hours of operation.

How to get there: From Salida, take US 50 West for 3.9 miles and turn left onto US 285 South. Drive 26.3 miles and turn left onto CO 17. Bear right to stay on CO 17 and continue 1.4 miles, then turn left onto CR 58EE; Joyful Journey Hot Springs is on the right.

OVERVIEW

The open-air soaking pools at Joyful Journey Mineral Hot Springs Spa are surrounded by wooden decks and protected from the elements with windscreens looking out on the Sangre de Cristo Mountains. The peaceful setting, along with a unique variety of overnight accommodations—a lodge, yurt village, and tepees—and plethora of spa treatments may tempt the day-soaker into an extended stay, with the promise of sleeping late and enjoying a continental breakfast before giving in to a long massage, scrub, or body wrap, aromatherapy session, and sauna, or simply a long open-air soak in a mineral-rich hot pool.

The Hot Springs

Three outdoor soaking pools set in wooden decking are surrounded by Plexiglas windscreens, offering views of the Sangre de Cristo Mountains. Overhead canopies stretched high above the pools provide protection from showers and a reprieve from the intense high-altitude rays of the sun. The smallest and deepest of the three, the Tower Pool, is maintained at 104°. The Cool Pool is 3.5 feet deep and 98° to 100°. Across a boardwalk lies the Hot Pool, filled with 106° to 108° hot spring water.

For a private soak, reserve an indoor hot mineral tub. Pools and tubs are brimming with hot mineral water that's gravity-fed from the on-site artesian well. Joyful Journey uses no chemicals and no recirculation.

Top: Hot springs soaking meets snow-capped mountains at Joyful Journey Hot Springs Spa.
Bottom: Joyful Journey's Tower Pool is the deepest of three outdoor soaking pools.
PHOTOS BY STEWART M. GREEN

The Site

Joyful Journey Mineral Hot Springs Spa is a well-appointed relaxation destination. Along with the soaking pools and tubs, there's a sauna and changing rooms, showers, plus bathing suits, towels, and lockers available for rent. An eleven-room motel lodge with private bathrooms and a large conference center with kitchen facilities attract families, clubs, and business groups for special events, reunions, and retreats. There's even a nondenominational minister on staff available for weddings, and an aromatherapist.

If private bathrooms and indoor plumbing aren't your style, you can opt for a yurt or a tepee with shared community bathrooms. The yurts are heated, have electricity, and come with beds and bedding, while the tepees have platforms for your sleeping bags and mats. The spa at Joyful Journey offers a variety of luxurious body and facial treatments that include massage, reflexology, skin-soothing wraps, and exfoliating scrubs. Choose from a line of in-house products for your spa treatments. There's a small spa shop where you can buy home treatments and refreshments.

Hot Springs History

European settlers began bathing here around 1892. The area served as a settlement in the early expansion of the American West. Like other hot springs in the area, Mineral Hot Springs, now known as Joyful Journey, served as a commune of sorts for those seeking an alternative lifestyle. Eventually the property became a private, family-owned business and was developed into the current retreat.

Area Highlights

Joyful Journey's proximity to the Sangre de Cristo Mountains and San Isabel and Rio Grande National Forests offers plenty of outdoor adventures like hiking and camping. Mountaineers note that just 25 miles to the southeast lies the town of Crestone and the Willow Lake Trailhead, providing access to the 14,000-foot peaks Kit Carson Mountain and Challenger Point. Easier day hikes in the area—such as the North Crestone Loop Trail—are found at the North Crestone Lake Trailhead, or take the Willow Lake Trail up to Willow Park or Willow Lake and choose your own turn-around point. Rock climbers need venture just 45 miles southwest of Joyful Journey to Penitente Canyon, the best climbing area in the San Luis Valley. For a relaxing and scenic driving tour, head south on CO 17 to pick up the Los Caminos Antiguos Scenic Byway. This 152-mile open loop crosses the San Luis Valley from Alamosa to Cumbres Pass, with plenty of scenery and historic stopping points along the way.

Be sure to fill the gas tank and pick up some groceries before heading back to Joyful Journey Mineral Hot Springs, for a cookout or cook-in. Enjoy an evening soak before you retire to your tepee for the night, and fall asleep under the stars in Colorado's tranquil San Luis Valley.

10. **SAND DUNES RECREATION**

Type: Family-oriented outdoor and indoor public swimming and soaking, adults-only bar, sauna, and soaking area, plus lodging.

Location: Hooper, about 25 miles north of Alamosa.

When to visit: Open year-round except Thursday for pool draining and cleaning, and for 10 days each April for maintenance.

Access: Year-round vehicle access on public roads. Call ahead for ADA access details.

Accommodations: 4 cabins; RV sites with electric and water hookups, plus dry sites and dump station; tent camping.

Rules: Day-soakers welcome. Clothing is required. No smoking. Pets allowed on leash or in kennel, but not allowed in the Greenhouse.

Services: Limited services in Hooper and nearby Mosca; full services 24 miles south in Alamosa.

Map & GPS: *DeLorme: Colorado Atlas & Gazetteer*: p. 80, C4; 37.779042 / -105.856445.

Contact: Sand Dunes Recreation, 1991 CR 63, Hooper, CO 81136; (719) 378-2807; http://sanddunespool.com. Call or visit website for rates, reservations, and hours of operation.

How to get there: From Salida, take US 50 West for 3.9 miles and turn left onto US 285 South. Drive 26.3 miles and turn left onto CO 17. Bear right to stay on CO 17 and continue 29.4 miles. Turn left on CR B and go 1.5 miles, then turn left on CR 63 and go 1 mile to Sand Dunes Recreation.

OVERVIEW

Sand Dunes Recreation is a lively hot spring center with something for everyone. Swim, soak, eat, lounge on the patio, or grab a cold beer or glass of wine at the bar. The development is not what you would expect in a town known for UFO sightings, and it's definitely worth the drive.

The Hot Springs

The centerpiece here is the big outdoor pool with sundecks and chairs, a fountain, diving board, and magnificent views of Great Sand Dunes National Park and the Sierra Blanca Range. The pool is 98° to 100°, and the west end extends into a covered greenhouse area with a partition and adjoining 1-foot-deep kiddie pool. Indoors, a 3,500-gallon, 105° to 107° therapeutic pool accommodates up to twenty-five soakers.

The newest addition is the adults-only, 10,000-square-foot Greenhouse, where you have four soaking options: the Coffin Tub is 110.5°, the Deep Thought Tub is 107°, the 103 Tub is—you guessed it—103°, and the Zero Entry Pool is 98°. The sauna seats ten people.

The Site

Sand Dunes Recreation has long been a local hot spot for families and teens. The Mile Deep Grille offers a full menu, and you can enjoy your meal indoors at a picnic table or take it outside to a nice area past the pool. Here, the land drops off a bit, providing a natural separation between the pool and a pleasant, creekside grassy area with a volleyball net, horseshoe pits, fire pit, tables, chairs, and grills.

The Greenhouse is the place to be for adults. Eat on the patio, have a beer or glass of wine on the deck, or enjoy a hot soak in a tub or pool, followed up with a cool mist spray. The Greenhouse is 70° year-round and beautifully decorated with paving stones, flowers, and lush greenery.

There's plenty of lodging too. Tent sites feature picnic tables, grass, fire pits, and parking; ten RV sites have electric and water hookups; and there are ten more dry sites. Three small cabins offer a glamping experience, with electricity and fire pits, plus a foot pump sink, portable toilet, and access to communal bathrooms and shower house. The larger Hooper Hacienda has a full kitchen, two private baths, and a fire pit, and sleeps ten.

Rounding out Sand Dunes Recreation are changing areas, swim lessons, water-aerobics classes, weekly light shows, and a gift shop where you can buy or rent pool toys and more.

Hot Springs History

Drilled in the early 1930s as an exploratory oil well, the artesian hot spring well at Sand Dunes Pool now provides 118° sulfur-free water to the facility at 1,200 gallons per minute. The site was initially developed as a swimming area but suffered through

Below: Enjoy adults-only soaking in the Greenhouse at Sand Dunes Recreation.
Facing page: Sand Dunes Recreation is popular year-round for swimming, soaking, and sunning.
PHOTOS BY STEWART M. GREEN

Enjoy the hot spring spray at Sand Dunes Recreation. STEWART M. GREEN

extended periods of disuse over the years. Sharie and Ed Harmon brought the facility to its current clean and comfortable state, and it's impeccably run by daughter Carly Harmon and her husband, Donnie Bautista.

Area Highlights
With affordable RV and tent sites, cabins, and on-site food and beverages, Sand Dunes Recreation makes a good home base for exploring Alamosa County and the San Luis Valley. A 24-mile drive southeast brings you to Great Sand Dunes National Park and the tallest sand dune—base to tip—in North America. Board the dunes, or just hike around and enjoy views of the Crestones, a striking collection of 14,000-foot-high peaks to the north.

Many more miles of hiking and biking trails await you in the Rio Grande and San Isabel National Forests, and you can pick up a map at US Forest Service offices in Saguache or Del Norte. Finish the day with hot pizza and a cold drink at Mile Deep Grille, and a good night's sleep in your cabin, RV, or tent at the Sand Dunes Pool.

11. COLORADO GATORS REPTILE PARK

Type: Rustic outdoor and indoor public reptile rescue—not for human soaking.

Location: Mosca, about 17 miles north of Alamosa.

When to visit: 7 days a week year-round EXCEPT closed on Thanksgiving and Christmas.

Access: Year-round vehicle access on public roads. Call ahead for ADA access details.

Accommodations: None on-site, but tent camping is located at nearby UFO WatchTower and Campground; camping, RV sites, and lodging are available at nearby Sand Dunes Recreation in Hooper. Additional accommodations are located 17 miles south in Alamosa.

Rules: No soaking—hot springs are for alligators only. No smoking. Pets are allowed, either carried or on leash.

Services: Limited services in Mosca and nearby Hooper; full services 17 miles south in Alamosa.

Map & GPS: *DeLorme: Colorado Atlas & Gazetteer:* p. 80, C4; 37.705995 / -105.870250.

Contact: Colorado Gators Reptile Park, 9162 CR 9 N, Mosca, CO 81146; (719) 378-2612; www.coloradogators .com; email: colog8rs@gmail.com. Call or visit website for rates and hours of operation.

How to get there: From Salida, take US 50 West for 3.9 miles and turn left onto US 285 South. Drive 26.3 miles and turn left onto CO 17. Bear right to stay on CO 17 and continue 33.4 miles, then turn left onto Ninemile Lane and continue 0.2 mile to Lane 9 North. Go 0.2 mile to Colorado Gators Reptile Park, on the right.

OVERVIEW

Natural hot springs are generally reserved for soaking and swimming, but you wouldn't dip your toes into this San Luis Valley thermal pool—the waters are infested with alligators.

The Hot Springs

Colorado Gators Reptile Park is an animal refuge and home to more than 200 alligators—nearly all rescues—as well as crocodiles, rattlesnakes, pythons, turtles, and other animals that outgrew their previous owners' interests or abilities to care for them. The overflow from the hot spring pools—which is 87° at the source and cools to about 70°, depending on the season—is funneled into Two Mile Creek. The waters spread over a 37-acre wetlands area and wildlife habitat, and more than a hundred species of wild birds have been spotted on the premises.

The Site

The stars of these hot springs are the animals that have found sanctuary in the exotic animal rescue. There are indoor aquariums filled with snakes, turtles, and other reptiles, outdoor pools of baby alligators, and fenced-in areas with tall emus. Brilliant peacocks and sturdy box turtles wander the grounds, and bright-colored wild birds dot

Above: Visit the wildlife habitat at Colorado Gators Reptile Park.

Left: Hot spring waters at Colorado Gators Reptile Park are the perfect habitat for alligators. PHOTOS BY STEWART M. GREEN

the grasslands. There's a creek where you can paddle a boat, and if you catch a carp, you can feed it to the alligators. Colorado Gators Reptile Park offers alligator- and reptile-handling classes and provides educational programs to area schools and clubs, and you can pick up a cool alligator souvenir in the gift shop.

Hot Springs History

The 80-acre property at Colorado Gators Reptile Park was purchased by Erwin and Lynne Young in 1977 specifically for raising tilapia. A decade later, they purchased one hundred baby alligators as an eco-friendly addition to help dispose of the aquacultural waste. In 1990, they opened the park to visitors, mostly locals eager to view the

Above: Hundreds of alligators make Colorado Gators Reptile Park their home. Below: Colorado Gators Reptile Park is an animal rescue for reptiles. PHOTOS BY STEWART M. GREEN

growing reptiles. As interest in the unusual environment grew, so did the crowds, who saw the property as a good place to drop off their unwanted reptile pets. Today, Erwin and Lynne, along with their children, grandchildren, and daughter-in-law, continue to own and operate the fish farm, reptile park, and animal sanctuary, attracting visitors from across the state.

Area Highlights

The Colorado Gators Reptile Park is a fun side trip for families visiting nearby Great Sand Dunes National Park for camping and hiking, Sand Dunes Recreation for soaking, or Penitente Canyon for camping, hiking, and rock climbing.

Just a few miles south in Alamosa, visit the Alamosa National Wildlife Refuge complex, which provides a safe breeding and feeding habitat for hundreds of bird species, including the rare whooping crane. While you're in town, check out San Luis Lakes State Wildlife Area, Alamosa Ranch & Open Space Wildlife Viewing Area, and Blanca Vista Park, with hiking and biking trails, picnic areas, and lots of wildlife viewing. Or take a ride on the Rio Grande Scenic Railroad to the old town of La Veta, where there's shopping, museums, and restaurants to visit before you climb back aboard for the return trip. Just don't buy any alligators—contrary to what you may have heard, they do not make good pets, and you can always get your gator fix back at Colorado Gators Reptile Park.

12. SPLASHLAND

Type: Family-oriented outdoor public swimming.

Location: Alamosa, about 80 miles south of Salida.

When to visit: Open seasonally, Tuesday through Sunday from Memorial Day weekend through Labor Day. Also open for school trips from May through October—call for details.

Access: Year-round vehicle access on public roads. ADA access throughout.

Accommodations: None on-site, but tent camping, RV parks, and motels are located in Alamosa.

Rules: Day-soaker facility. Clothing is required. No smoking, alcohol, or glass containers. Service pets only.

Services: Full services in Alamosa.

Map & GPS: *DeLorme: Colorado Atlas & Gazetteer:* p. 80, E4; 37.488983 / -105.858448.

Contact: Splashland, 5895 CO 17, Alamosa, CO 81101; (719) 589-6258; www.splashlandllc.com. Call or visit website for rates and hours of operation.

How to get there: In Alamosa, take US 160 East and turn left onto CO 17. Continue 1.1 miles to Splashland, on the left.

OVERVIEW

Splashland is as simple and straightforward a hot springs site as you could hope for, and maybe that's what's so great about it. One ginormous outdoor pool and an indoor snack bar make for the perfect family fun center, and you won't lose the kids.

Splashland has reopened after a hiatus. STEWART M. GREEN

Top: Splashland in Alamosa is a seasonal hot spring but worth the wait.
Bottom: Two big slides and a kiddie slide make Splashland a fun place for kids.
PHOTOS BY STEWART M. GREEN

The Hot Springs

At 60 feet wide and 150 feet long, Splashland's big geothermal swimming pool is the biggest outdoor pool in the San Luis Valley and one of the largest hot springs pools in the state. Water is 102° at the source and 92° to 96° in the pool, and the depth ranges from 3 to 10 feet. There's a diving board, lap lanes, two 50-foot slides and a kiddie slide, and enough wraparound concrete decks to find your place in the sun.

The Site

The layout at Splashland is simple, with big, clean, changing rooms and lockers—men's on one side and women's on the other—and a snack bar in the middle. Order some barbecue or rent a grill and cook your own. Goggles, floaties, suits, towels, and pool toys are available to rent or purchase. There's a warming hut, picnic area, and shade canopies, and the site is available to rent for all your special events. This is one of the few hot springs with a chair-to-pool hydraulic lift for wheelchairs, plus an ADA-friendly shower and changing area.

Splashland is a community-minded place, with lots of activities, competitions, and events, from triathlons to lifeguarding classes, and early-morning lap swims to SilverSneakers Splash programs for seniors.

Hot Springs History

Like all the other hot springs in the San Luis Valley, Splashland was a serendipitous find when oil drillers turned up water instead of oil. The pool opened for the first time in 1955. After closing for several years, the site was remodeled and reopened in 2014, to the delight of Alamosans and visitors to the area.

Area Highlights

Visit the San Luis Valley History Museum or enjoy the Alamosa Historic Walking Tour. In June, Alamosa hosts SummerFest on the Rio, a festival with arts and crafts, food, music, and more.

Finally, from May through October, drive 28 miles south to Antonito and catch a ride on the Cumbres & Toltec Scenic Railroad. The nineteenth-century steam engine travels across the state line to Chama, New Mexico. With 64 miles of track running through gorges and tunnels, over trestles and passes, you'll understand why thirteen movies have been filmed on the Cumbres & Toltec Scenic Railroad. Bring binoculars for wildlife viewing in summer and leaf peeping in the fall. You can finish the day with some hot food and a warm dip at your favorite hot springs pool, Splashland.

CENTRAL ROCKIES COLORADO HOT SPRINGS

BUENA VISTA, NATHROP, SALIDA, GUNNISON COUNTY, ASPEN, REDSTONE, AND GLENWOOD SPRINGS

The central Rockies host a variety of hot spring options from sprawling public resorts to quiet adults-only soaking pools and roadside and wilderness wild springs. The area boasts the largest indoor hot springs pool in the state, the only natural hot springs vapor caves in North America, and the largest outdoor hot springs pool in the world. They're all located within a 2- to 4-hour drive from Denver and Colorado Springs.

Three cascading pools of varying temperatures tempt the soaker and the swimmer at Avalanche Ranch Cabins & Hot Springs.
STEWART M. GREEN

13. COTTONWOOD HOT SPRINGS INN & SPA

Type: Rustic, quiet outdoor public and private soaking and spa services, plus lodging.

Location: Buena Vista, about 25 miles north of Salida.

When to visit: 7 days a week year-round.

Access: Year-round vehicle access on public roads. ADA access to some cabins and 1 lodge room.

Accommodations: 13-room lodge, 4 private creek-side cabins with soaking pools, 1 private cabin (no pool), 3-bedroom private guesthouse, 2 dormitories, and tent camping.

Rules: Day-soakers welcome. Clothing is required. No drugs, including marijuana, and no alcohol. No glass or pets in pool area, and no pets in the lodge (in cabins and tent sites only). Smoking in designated area only, away from pools.

Services: Full services in Buena Vista.

Map & GPS: *DeLorme: Colorado Atlas & Gazetteer:* p. 60, B1; 38.812660 / -106.222322.

Contact: Cottonwood Hot Springs Inn & Spa, 18999 CR 306, Buena Vista, CO 81211; (719) 395-6434; http://cotton wood-hot-springs.com/colorado. Call or visit website for rates, reservations, and hours of operation.

How to get there: In Buena Vista, go west on Main Street to CO 306 and drive 4.6 miles. Turn right, to Cottonwood Hot Springs, on the left.

OVERVIEW

Fourteen miles east of the Continental Divide, Cottonwood Hot Springs Inn & Spa sits along the banks of Cottonwood Creek, surrounded by the San Isabel National Forest. The Collegiate Peaks hover to the north and south, and somewhere in between, tucked in a tangle of cottonwood trees, hot springs gurgle and bubble and babble and seep their way from deep beneath the earth up to the surface, filling pools of natural stone with crystal clear, hot mineral water. Cottonwood Hot Springs is a secret sanctuary of meditation and healing, nestled in the wilderness and hidden in plain sight.

The Hot Springs

Five outdoor soaking pools cluster on the north side of Cottonwood Creek. At the center, the Belly Pool is about 45 feet long by 20 feet wide and 5 feet deep in the center. To the northwest and adjoining the Belly Pool is the Head Pool, and south of the Head Pool is the L-shaped Elbow Pool, surrounded by rocks and greenery and partially covered with a canvas awning for shade. East of the Elbow Pool lies the Watsu, and the fifth pool is the slightly cooler Cold Pool. Each pool is made of natural river rock and contains pure, natural gravity-fed spring water with no chlorine or chemicals added. There are changing rooms with hot showers and a dry sauna. Private outdoor soaking pools accompany three of the overnight cabins. The source waters at Cottonwood Hot Springs range from 132° to 150°, and the pools are maintained at a comfortable 90° to 110°.

Cottonwood Hot Springs Inn & Spa lies along Cottonwood Creek in Buena Vista.
STEWART M. GREEN

The Site

There's an eclectic mix of lodging at Cottonwood, including a motel-style lodge, women's-only and coed dorms, rustic cabins, a guesthouse, and tent campsites. There are no phones, TV, Wi-Fi, or air-conditioning in the rooms. Lodge rooms have ceiling fans, and the cabins have full kitchens, charcoal grills, and private bathrooms. For overnight stays, it's a good idea to call ahead for reservations, especially in the busy summertime. A basic continental breakfast is offered each morning, and donations are appreciated.

The operative words here are "harmony, healing, growth, rejuvenation, and restoration," a philosophy supported by unique therapies and other spiritual offerings. Cottonwood Hot Springs does not allow alcohol, marijuana, or other drugs on the premises. The management here is particularly adamant about this restriction, due to health risks and the potentially adverse effects of alcohol on the mind, body, and spirit, a state in direct opposition to the hot springs' positive intentions and benefits.

Hot Springs History

Development at Cottonwood dates back to 1878, when Reverend Adams and his wife, Dr. J. A. D. Adams, built a hotel on the site. Dr. Adams practiced medicine here, and the hot springs at Cottonwood were used for drinking, bathing, and to treat ailments such as catarrh, dyspepsia, and rheumatism. The hotel burned in 1911 and was never rebuilt. After changing hands several times, the property came under the ownership of current proprietor Cathy Manning, who has run the place for more than thirty years.

Five outdoor pools provide quiet soaking at Cottonwood Hot Springs. Day-soakers are welcome. PHOTOS BY STEWART M. GREEN

You can always find a peaceful spot at Cottonwood Hot Springs Inn & Spa.
STEWART M. GREEN

Area Highlights

Buena Vista is peak-central for folks looking to get up fifteen of Colorado's many 14,000-foot peaks. Trailheads to peaks in the Sawatch Range are all located within an hour's drive of the hot springs. Many Coloradoans head to Buena Vista to gas up, eat up, and sometimes bed down before and after a big day in the mountains.

This is also a popular spot for whitewater rafting, kayaking, and paddleboarding, with the Arkansas River running through town and plenty of outfitters ready to take you out on the waters. For mountain biking, head to the Midland Railroad Grade, a 14.6-mile out-and-back that takes advantage of an old railroad grade for an interesting and easy ride, combining dirt road and single-track with great views of Mount Princeton and the southern Arkansas Valley. For a shorter trip, check out Buena Vista River Park; for a longer one, try out the 18.6-mile Buena Vista River Road. Experienced bikers can head over to the Colorado Trail, where they can test their technical riding skills on the 16.8-mile out-and-back trip from Mount Princeton to South Cottonwood Creek.

For a scenic drive, go west to Cottonwood Pass. For a shorter trip, head east into downtown Buena Vista and then north, through the Midland Train Tunnels to Elephant Rock. Buena Vista's mining and railroad histories are evident all over town, but wherever you go and however you get there, the soothing waters at Cottonwood Hot Springs Inn & Spa are still just a stone's throw away.

14. MOUNT PRINCETON HOT SPRINGS RESORT

Type: Family-oriented, resort-style outdoor public swimming, soaking, and spa services, plus lodging and fitness center.

Location: Nathrop, about 8 miles south of Buena Vista.

When to visit: 7 days a week year-round.

Access: Year-round vehicle access on public roads. Call ahead for ADA access details.

Accommodations: 49 rooms total in 3 lodges, plus 30 private cabins and RV parking but no hookups.

Rules: Day-soakers welcome. Clothing is required. No alcohol in the pool areas, no smoking, no pets.

Services: Full services in nearby Buena Vista.

Map & GPS: *DeLorme: Colorado Atlas & Gazetteer:* p. 60, C1; 38.732799 / -106.161371.

Contact: Mount Princeton Hot Springs Resort, 15870 CR 162, Nathrop, CO 81236; (719) 395-2447; https://mtprinceton.com. Call or visit website for rates, reservations, and hours of operation.

How to get there: From Buena Vista, take US 24 East for 2.4 miles and get on US 285 South. Drive 5.6 miles and turn right onto CR 162/Chalk Creek Drive. Go 4.4 miles to Mount Princeton Hot Springs, on the left.

OVERVIEW

In a state brimming with hot spring swimming pools, soaking pools, creekside pools, lodges, cabins, spas, and mountain views, one hot springs location has it all. Mount Princeton Hot Springs Resort sits at the base of some of the highest summits in Colorado, in an area surrounded by nearly a quarter of the state's 14,000-foot peaks, by the mouth of a canyon, with a creek rushing through and wilderness all around. All that, and it's just 4 miles from a national highway. Throw in a country store, bar and restaurant, and access to just about every outdoor recreational activity for which Colorado is known, and you've got a hot spring destination with something for everyone.

The Hot Springs

The hot springs here produce 175,000 gallons of 130° water every day, filling nine swimming and soaking pools and tubs and thirty in-creek pools. The Exercise (Lap) Pool is located near the bathhouse and kept at a tepid 90°, ideal for swimming and water play. Nearby is the Soaking Pool, a much hotter 100°. Both pools are located in sunny spots with long concrete decks. A quieter, shady alternative is a series of three Cascading Pools, with temperatures graduating from about 100° to 105°. The Exercise, Soaking, and Cascading Pools are open year-round and available for day-soakers. On the other side of the creek is the Relaxation Pool for adult (16 and older) overnight guests only. Access is gained via a bridge over Chalk Creek, where you can view about thirty natural pools scattered along the banks. The in-creek pools are also open for day-soakers, with access and temperatures dependent on water flow. The final pool, the Upper Pool, is open seasonally to overnight guests and day-soakers from

Mount Princeton Hot Springs Resort sits at the base of some of the highest summits in Colorado.
COURTESY MOUNT PRINCETON HOT SPRINGS

Memorial Day weekend through Labor Day. This is a very large swimming pool with an adjoining Kiddie Pool, hot tub, and lazy river.

The Site

The setting and location at Mount Princeton Hot Springs are hard to top; there's just no other resort in the state that's managed to get this close to so many big peaks! Your reward is stunning mountain views from just about everywhere on the site. The trade-off, as with any of Colorado's large hot springs establishments, is the popularity of the place. However, much of the new development here has been spread about and protected with dividing fences and natural borders, so you can still get some privacy if you're willing to wander a bit.

There are three separate lodges at Mount Princeton and many private cabins. The Main Lodge is convenient to the six lower pools (Exercise, Soaking, Relaxation, and three Cascading) and all the pools in the creek, and the building also houses a bar and restaurant. From here, it's a very short walk to the Country Store, the Pavilion (event center), and a new 14,000-square-foot spa. Keep in mind that this is not a place for high heels. Wear comfortable shoes and enjoy the lovely trails that connect the hotels with the many accoutrements that Mount Princeton has to offer!

The Poolside Lodge is located near the upper pools—the big swimming pool, hot tub, Kiddie Pool, and lazy river, as well as the basketball and tennis courts. Since these pools are seasonal, the Poolside Lodge is a good choice for Memorial Day weekend through Labor Day, especially for families. This lodge is the closest one to the peaks, so you'll have the best views here too. You can walk to all the other pools from the Poolside Lodge, or drive from the upper to the lower parking lot.

To avoid the crowds, savor an evening soak at Mount Princeton Hot Springs. COURTESY MOUNT PRINCETON HOT SPRINGS

The Cliffside Lodge is more secluded, has private patios for each room, and gives you good views of the peaks and the entire resort below. Finally, there are many private cabins scattered about, and they are not rustic but rather on the high end of accommodations here. The interiors shine with gleaming wood from floor to vaulted ceiling, there are convenient kitchenettes with marble countertops, and each living space has a flat-screen TV, gas fireplace, iPod hookup, sound system, and DVD player.

In addition to lodging, Mount Princeton Hot Springs has a conference center for business meetings and a pavilion for special events. The conference center sits high on a northeast hillside, near one of the lodges and some of the cabins, while the pavilion is located in the southwest corner of the resort, near the Main Lodge and alongside a meadow on Chalk Creek. Guests here can spill out onto the lawn and enjoy sunlit gardens, shady picnic areas, and views of the chalk cliffs of Mount Princeton and surrounding peaks.

The Spa at Mount Princeton Resort offers facials, body wraps, massages, and just about every other treatment you can imagine. Mount Princeton Hot Springs Resort is surrounded by trails, mountains, canyons, and rivers, with all kinds of opportunities for adventure, so check with their concierge service to arrange the details of those activities for you.

Hot Springs History

D. H. Heywood did the original government survey here and took ownership of the hot springs property as payment for his labor. The stage station, freight depot, and hotel that were built overlooked what is now the bathhouse, where some of the numerous springs bubble from the ground. Later, as the Mary Murphy Mine spawned greater wealth, a consortium of miners and businessmen built a grand three-story-tall hotel. A millionaire from Kansas City named J. C. Gafford anted up the money to build a magnificent four-story hotel. Exotic woods from all over the world and more than a hundred rooms made up this showpiece. There was custom monogrammed silverware, a freight elevator, and even a crude intercom system. Impressive grounds with stonework and ponds, enclosed hot pools, and a golf course made a splendid display of wealth, but they, too, were destined to fall into disrepair when the Mary Murphy closed in 1924 and the last railroad pulled out. An extensive assortment of owners and foreclosures followed, and the old hotel woodwork ended up in a housing development in Texas. Finally, in 1960 new owner Dennis Osborn began

The Exercise (Lap) Pool is ideal for swimming and water play. STEWART M. GREEN

building the series of pools and a lodge that still remain today, and in 2005 Mount Princeton Holdings LLC took ownership of the property and has since made major investments in the area, promising to restore Mount Princeton Hot Springs Resort to its earlier days of grandeur.

Area Highlights

The concierge service at Mount Princeton can make recommendations for your group and set up trips for you, too, or you can do this yourself. For downhill skiing and snowboarding, Monarch Mountain Ski Area is less than an hour's drive to the southwest on Monarch Pass, or you can head north to Ski Cooper in Leadville. There's kayaking and whitewater rafting on the Arkansas River at Brown's Canyon to the east, and four-wheeling to the west in St. Elmo. Local outfitters can provide the gear, instruction, and guide services for all of these activities, but you may want to pack the right kind of footwear and clothing, some sunscreen, and a water bottle for all of your outings. There are miles of trails around the hot springs for hiking or biking in summer and snowshoeing or Nordic skiing in winter. There's even a stable nearby for horseback-riding trips into the mountains for an hour, a day, or overnight, with campfires and quiet nights under the stars. Of course, you can always head back to Mount Princeton Hot Springs Resort for a midmorning soak in the Cascading Pools and a fruit and cheese platter, washed down with some sparkling water and topped off with a long nap.

15. ANTERO HOT SPRING CABINS

Type: Outdoor private soaking with vacation rental lodging.

Location: Nathrop, about 8 miles south of Buena Vista.

When to visit: 7 days a week year-round by reservation only.

Access: Year-round vehicle access on public roads.

Accommodations: Two early twentieth-century cabins and a split-level home, all with fully equipped kitchens and indoor bathrooms.

Rules: No day-soakers. Pools are for cabin guests only, so clothing is optional. No smoking, no pets.

Services: Full services in nearby Buena Vista.

Map & GPS: *DeLorme: Colorado Atlas & Gazetteer*: p. 60, C1; 38.731621 / -106.167141.

Contact: Antero Hot Spring Cabins, 16120 CR 162, Nathrop, CO 81236; (719) 539-8204; http://antero hotsprings.com. Call or visit website for rates and reservations.

How to get there: From Buena Vista, take US 24 East for 2.4 miles and get on US 285 South. Drive 5.6 miles and turn right onto CR 162/Chalk Creek Drive. Go 4.6 miles to Antero Hot Spring, on the left.

OVERVIEW

Several vacation rentals in Nathrop offer quiet, comfortable stays and private hot springs pools.

Two early twentieth-century cabins and a newer single-family home—each with its own hot spring pool—make up Antero Hot Spring Cabins. While each private rental enjoys its own quaint charm, the real draw is their location on Chalk Creek, at the foot of Mount Princeton and Mount Antero, and a short walk from Mount Princeton Hot Springs Resort.

The Hot Springs

Hand-formed concrete pools are enclosed by fencing for privacy and filled with hot spring water. While the source water is 120°, the pools are maintained at 102° to 104°, and a valve provides cold well water to further adjust the temperature. Each pool is drained and cleaned between each stay, and no chemicals are added.

The Site

The square-cut timber-built Cottonwood Cabin was built in the early 1900s and moved to its current location by horse train around 1920. It once served as a combination post office–schoolhouse. The cabin has been updated with indoor plumbing and a fully equipped kitchen and sleeps four. A white quartz fireplace in the living room was hand-built by the cabin's earlier owner, Alma Cowgill.

The slightly larger Hortense Cabin was built in 1926. Like the Cottonwood, this cabin has been updated and retains its Old West charm with much of the original

Facing page: Enjoy a private soak in your own hot springs pool at Antero Hot Spring Cabins a few feet from Chalk Creek. STEWART M. GREEN

Top: Three vacation rentals at Antero Hot Spring Cabins offer lots of choices, and each one has its own soaking pool. Bottom: The cabins at Antero Hot Spring are clean, cozy, and unique.
PHOTOS BY STEWART M. GREEN

interior intact. There's a wood stove for heat, and it sleeps six. In 2004, new owners took great care to have the Cottonwood and Hortense recaulked and refurbished for comfort, while keeping the original elements intact for aesthetic, as well as historic, reasons.

The Chalk Cliffs Chalet is more modern and sits on 2 acres of land. Accommodating up to ten people, the Chalet is popular for retreats, clubs, and family get-togethers, and there's plenty of room to spread out between the chalet, soaking pool, and the creek.

Not all cabins have Wi-Fi or air-conditioning, but they all have barbecue grills, picnic tables, and fireplaces, and guests are provided with firewood from October to April.

16. ALPINE HOT SPRINGS HIDEAWAY

Type: Outdoor private swiming and soaking with vacation rental lodging.

Location: Nathrop, about 8 miles south of Buena Vista.

When to visit: 7 days a week year-round by reservation only.

Access: Year-round vehicle access on public roads.

Accommodations: Mountain home sleeps 10. Fully equipped kitchen and indoor bathrooms.

Rules: No day-soakers. Pool is for vacation home renters only, so clothing is optional. No smoking indoors; service pets only.

Services: Full services in nearby Buena Vista.

Map & GPS: *DeLorme: Colorado Atlas & Gazetteer:* p. 60, C1; 38.733025 / -106.168844.

Contact: Alpine Hot Springs Hideaway, 16185 CR 162, Nathrop, CO 81236, (719) 530-1112; www.alpine hotsprings.com. Call or visit website for rates and reservations.

How to get there: From Buena Vista, take US 24 East for 2.4 miles and get on US 285 South. Drive 5.6 miles and turn right onto CR 162/Chalk Creek Drive. Go 4.7 miles to Alpine Hot Springs Hideaway, on the right.

OVERVIEW

What could be better than your own hot spring pool in the San Isabel National Forest? This private soaking pool and vacation rental is located on an acre of land near the Collegiate Peaks and Mount Princeton Hot Springs Resort.

Alpine Hot Springs Hideaway is located near the beautiful chalk cliffs at Mount Antero.
STEWART M. GREEN

Alpine Hot Springs Hideaway is a vacation rental with its own private hot springs swimming and soaking pool. STEWART M. GREEN

The Hot Springs

A large, 4-foot-deep backyard hot springs pool was hand-built by previous owners and fits twelve people comfortably. Between soaks, relax on the deck and listen to a babbling creek that runs through the property. The hot spring source water, which comes from the same aquifer as nearby Mount Princeton Hot Springs Resort, is 130° and cooled to 98° for the pool, but it's adjustable up or down with cooling tanks. The pool is cleaned between guests, and no chemicals are added.

The Site

The rustic vacation home at Alpine Hot Springs Hideaway belies a modern interior with all the amenities. Three bedrooms, two bathrooms, and two pullouts accommodate ten people comfortably, while three big screen TVs, plus high-speed internet and Wi-Fi make this a comfortable retreat. Cook your meals in the full kitchen—which has everything you need except the food—and eat in the dining room, or dine on one of two decks, with stunning views of the surrounding backcountry and 14,000-foot peaks. There's a gas grill, patio tables, and chairs. If you have a camper or several vehicles, the enormous private parking area will accommodate you.

Ask the owners, Craig and Tracie Cardwell, who have appeared on the Weather Channel's *Prospectors*, about mineral tours and gemstone hunting on nearby Mount Antero. Tracie also has a line of handmade gemstone jewelry and a skincare line sourced from local minerals.

17. TREEHOUSE HOT SPRINGS

Type: Outdoor private swiming and soaking with vacation rental lodging.

Location: Nathrop, about 8 miles south of Buena Vista.

When to visit: 7 days a week year-round by reservation only.

Access: Year-round vehicle access on public roads.

Accommodations: Creekside, elevated, octagon-shaped home sleeps 12, plus tent site. Fully equipped kitchen and indoor bathrooms.

Rules: No day-soakers. Pool is for guests only, so clothing is optional. No smoking indoors, no glass containers near the pool, and no pets allowed.

Services: Full services in nearby Buena Vista.

Map & GPS: *DeLorme: Colorado Atlas & Gazetteer*: p. 60, C1; 38.731052 / -106.172194.

Contact: Treehouse Hot Springs, 16790 CR 162, Nathrop, CO 81236; (719) 395-4474; www.treehouse-hotspring.com. Call or visit website for rates and reservations.

How to get there: From Buena Vista, take US 24 East for 2.4 miles and get on US 285 South. Drive 5.6 miles and turn right onto CR 162/Chalk Creek Drive. Go 4.9 miles to Treehouse Hot Springs, on the left.

OVERVIEW

Billed as "a little piece of heaven on Chalk Creek," Treehouse Hot Springs is a uniquely shaped house on 450 feet of creekside property.

Treehouse Hot Springs is tucked just off the road and along the creek in Chalk Creek Canyon.
STEWART M. GREEN

After a long day on the river, peaks, or trails, relax at the big hot springs pool at Treehouse Hot Springs. STEWART M. GREEN

The Hot Springs

One large hot springs pool is for vacation renters only at Treehouse Hot Springs. It's 27 feet long by 13 feet wide, slopes from 3 to 4 feet deep, and was recently refurbished with a sparkling-new, fiberglass bottom. The water is lightly chlorinated and the temperature is adjusted from 98.8° during the day to 100° to 101° at night. A privacy screen keeps out autumn leaves and winter breezes, and there's a shower and bathroom next to the pool.

The Site

The treehouse-style home, built in the mid-1980s, has five bedrooms, five bathrooms, and sleeps ten comfortably, although there's room for as many as fourteen people if you use the two couches for beds. The kitchen is fully equipped with everything except the food. There's also a laundry room, two gas fireplaces, and entertainment centers with lots of movies to watch. The big deck overlooks Chalk Creek, and there are three charcoal and propane barbecue grills, a picnic table, fire pit, and horseshoe pit. This is a popular site for family reunions, retreats, and group outings. Owners Harold and Judy Palmer live nearby in Nathrop and keep the place in great shape.

18. CREEKSIDE HOT SPRINGS CABIN

Type: Outdoor private soaking with vacation rental lodging.

Location: Nathrop, about 8 miles south of Buena Vista.

When to visit: 7 days a week year-round by reservation only.

Access: Year-round vehicle access on public roads. Call ahead for ADA access details.

Accommodations: Creekside mountain home sleeps 8. Fully equipped kitchen and indoor bathrooms.

Rules: No day-soakers. Pool is for guests only, so clothing is optional. No smoking inside; use the smoking receptacle outside. No glass in the pool area. Pets allowed on approval only and with a fee. No campfires.

Services: Full services in nearby Buena Vista. No Wi-Fi or TV on-site.

Map & GPS: *DeLorme: Colorado Atlas & Gazetteer:* p. 60, C1; 38.724771 / -106.174367.

Contact: Creekside Hot Springs Cabin, 15654 CR 289A, Nathrop, CO 81236; (719) 207-2100; www.creekside hotsprings.com. Call or visit website for rates and reservations.

How to get there: From Buena Vista, take US 24 East for 2.4 miles and get on US 285 South. Drive 5.6 miles and turn right onto CR 162/Chalk Creek Drive. Go 3.9 miles and turn left onto CR 289, then go 1.5 miles and turn right onto CR 289A. Continue 0.2 mile to Creekside Hot Springs.

OVERVIEW

A big mountain home on the south side of Chalk Creek has room for everyone and a hot spring pool too.

The Hot Springs

An outdoor soaking pool along Chalk Creek accompanies this vacation rental home. The free-form pool is tiled, has a fiberglass bottom, is surrounded by wooden decking, and holds 750 gallons of hot spring water that's 120° at the source and cooled to 104°, although the temperature can be adjusted up or down. The water, from an artesian well, flows through the pool constantly.

The Site

The chalet-style home sits on 2.5 acres of land on Chalk Creek. With three bedrooms, two full bathrooms, plus a full basement, the house sleeps eight comfortably but can accommodate up to ten. There's a laundry room, a wood-burning fireplace, a big deck with chairs overlooking the creek, a propane grill, and everything else you need for an extended stay.

Area Highlights for *Antero Hot Spring Cabins, Alpine Hot Springs Hideaway, Treehouse Hot Springs,* and *Creekside Hot Springs Cabin*

Vacation rentals in Nathrop are a good choice for a romantic getaway or a group retreat, and there are plenty of ways to enjoy the area during your stay in Chaffee County. The sprawling Mount Princeton Hot Springs Resort is only 0.25 mile away,

Creekside Hot Springs Cabin is one of several private vacation rentals in Nathrop. The free-form pool is just steps from Chalk Creek at Creekside Hot Springs Cabin. Enjoy solitude, or invite your friends. PHOTOS BY STEWART M. GREEN

The private soaking pool at Creekside Hot Springs Cabin is continuously refilled with fresh hot mineral water every couple of hours. STEWART M. GREEN

and a few miles farther down the road, Chalk Creek joins the Arkansas River at Brown's Canyon, where you can take advantage of kayaking and whitewater rafting. The Continental Divide Trail and Colorado Trail are just minutes away.

Nearby 14,000-foot peaks Mount Harvard, Mount Columbia, Mount Yale, and Mount Princeton to the north, and Mount Antero, Mount Shavano, and Tabeguache Peak to the south make this a popular area for mountaineering, backcountry skiing, snowshoeing, and snowmobiling. For downhill skiing and snowboarding, Monarch Mountain is less than an hour's drive away, southwest at Monarch Pass.

Finally, St. Elmo, a well-preserved ghost town, is just a short drive west into the canyon. You can wander the site or rent a vehicle at the General Store and drive the old mining roads. However you spend your time in Chaffee County, your own private hot spring pool will be waiting for you back at Antero Hot Spring Cabins, Alpine Hot Springs Hideaway, Treehouse Hot Springs, or Creekside Hot Springs Cabin.

19. **SALIDA HOT SPRINGS AQUATIC CENTER**

Type: Family-oriented, indoor public swimming and private soaking.

Location: Salida, about 25 miles south of Buena Vista.

When to visit: 7 days a week year-round.

Access: Year-round vehicle access on public roads. Call ahead for ADA access details.

Accommodations: None on-site, but tent camping, RV parks, and motels are located in Salida.

Rules: Day-soaker facility. Clothing is required in pool, but optional in private baths. No smoking, no alcohol, no pets.

Services: Full services in Salida.

Map & GPS: *DeLorme: Colorado Atlas & Gazetteer:* p. 60, E2; 38.525003 / -106.009510.

Contact: Salida Hot Springs Aquatic Center, 410 W. Rainbow Blvd., Salida, CO 81201; (719) 539-6738; http://salida rec.com. Call or visit website for rates and hours of operation.

How to get there: From Buena Vista, take US 24 East for 2.4 miles and get on US 285 South. Drive 21 miles and turn left onto US 285 South/US 50 East. Continue 0.5 mile and turn left onto US 50 East, then continue 3.7 miles to Salida Hot Springs, on the left.

OVERVIEW

Salida is a small town with a big heart and a swimming pool to match. Situated in the center of the state on US 50, Salida Hot Springs Aquatic Center provides the local community and visitors alike with a year-round swimming, soaking, and water sports recreational facility fit for a town of any size. All this is thanks to natural hot spring water that's piped in from a nearby source high in the mountains to the biggest indoor hot spring pool in North America.

The Hot Springs

The main pool ranges from 4 to 12 feet deep and features six 25-meter lap lanes and a diving board, and the water is maintained at 84° to 86°. Two of its six lanes are usually reserved for swimming laps, while the rest of the pool is for diving and water play. The adjoining pool has a zero-depth entry with a gradual slope to 4 feet deep. At 95° to 100°, and with several small fountains shooting into the air, this is a popular spot for soaking and for the kids.

The private baths are 105°, clothing-optional, and available for rent by the hour. The pools and baths are fed by hot spring water, and the communal pools are lightly chlorinated, while the private baths are chemical-free.

The Site

This is a busy place, with a full schedule of activities, including swim and exercise classes, kayak roll sessions, water volleyball, and a weekly Family Night with reduced rates. Showers, lockers, towels, and suits are all available to rent. The Salida Hot Springs Aquatic Center is also home to the Salida Cyclones Swim Team and the Salida

Top: Salida Hot Springs Aquatic Center is the largest indoor hot springs pool in North America.
Bottom: Lap lanes are reserved for swimmers at Salida Hot Springs Aquatic Center.
PHOTOS BY STEWART M. GREEN

Spartans High School Swim Team. However, no matter how busy the schedule—or full the pool—there is usually time and space for everyone and anyone else too. The addition of a chairlift for lowering wheelchair-bound swimmers and soakers into the pool is just one example of how the center strives to meet the needs of the entire community. The building itself makes use of floor-to-ceiling windows at each end to allow for plenty of natural light, a nice complement to the clear and odorless natural mineral waters of the pools.

Hot Springs History

The Salida Hot Springs Aquatic Center was built during the Great Depression for $160,000 as part of a 1937 federal Works Progress Administration project. In 1941, the City of Salida purchased the land and water rights to the hot springs source for $40,000. Located a few miles to the west in the Rocky Mountains around Poncha Springs, several hot spring sources provide the aquatic center with an endless water supply. The original pipeline has been replaced, and the water flows from 8,000 feet above sea level, delivering a steady supply of natural mineral water to the Salida Hot Springs Aquatic Center.

Area Highlights

Situated in the central Rockies of Colorado, Salida provides ready access to roughly a quarter of Colorado's fifty-four famed "fourteeners," or peaks that rise above 14,000 feet. The area attracts hikers, bikers, climbers, campers, and, yes, even hot spring soakers, from across the state and beyond. Visit the Arkansas River for whitewater rafting and kayaking, or enjoy alpine and cross-country skiing on high-altitude slopes and trails. If all that activity just wears you out, call on a local outfitter and book a relaxing horseback ride through Colorado's scenic Rocky Mountains, or take a zip-line tour through its equally scenic canyons. And if you really want to enjoy all those grand views without straining a single muscle, drive 20 miles west to Monarch Pass and take a tram ride to the top of the Continental Divide. Whatever you choose, you won't be disappointed, at least not by the views.

If you visit the Salida Hot Springs Aquatic Center in June, you'll want to check out FIBArk, America's oldest whitewater rafting event and Salida's unofficial kickoff to summer. Fueled by spring snow runoff from the high mountain peaks, the Arkansas River is the setting for a number of whitewater events, including a 26-mile downriver race on class III rapids from Salida to Cotopaxi, the longest race of its kind in America. FIBArk is generally a weeklong event, centered at Riverside Park and surrounded by a carnival, arts, crafts, a farmers' market, food, beer, music, clinics, contests, and, of course, lots of whitewater rafting. Whenever you visit Salida, there's plenty to see and do here, and the aquatic center is fully enclosed, so you'll always have a warm spot to come back to after a big day in the high country.

20. WAUNITA HOT SPRINGS RANCH

Type: Family-oriented outdoor public swimming and soaking, plus lodging, or private outdoor swimming and soaking with vacation rental lodging.

Location: Gunnison County, about 27 miles east of Gunnison.

When to visit: 7 days a week year-round. Reservations recommended.

Access: Year-round vehicle access on public roads. Call ahead for ADA access details.

Accommodations: 2 lodges accommodating about 40 people total.

Rules: Day-soakers welcome in the off-season only; pools reserved for lodging guests during the summer months. Clothing is required. No smoking in the rooms or at the pools, and no pets.

Services: Full services in nearby Gunnison.

Map & GPS: *DeLorme: Colorado Atlas & Gazetteer*: p. 59, E6; 38.514582 / -106.507865.

Contact: Waunita Hot Springs Ranch, 8007 CR 887, Gunnison, CO 81230; (970) 641-1266; www.waunita.com. Call or visit website for rates, reservations, and hours of operation.

How to get there: From Gunnison, take US 50 East for about 18 miles and turn left onto CR 887. Go 8.1 miles and turn left to Waunita Hot Springs.

OVERVIEW

There are places you go as a child—long drives on bumpy roads that turn onto gravelly driveways. Traffic sounds give way to twittering birds, and you hear the clucks of chickens, whinny of a horse, or bleat of a goat announcing your arrival. You roll down the window and breathe in the smells. Complex and earthy, they tickle your nose with a sweet mix of hay and freshwater from a babbling brook that's cold and full of fish. There's a farmhouse with a long porch and chairs, and you can't wait to go inside, because you know the kitchen smells like cookies and pie, and you're going to drink lemonade on that porch tonight and sleep with the windows open. This is Waunita Hot Springs Ranch.

The Hot Springs

Waunita Hot Springs Ranch is a vacation rental first, but the swimming pool and soaking tub are open to day-soakers and overnight guests in the off-season. The hottest natural springs in the state are sourced from nearby 11,465-foot Tomichi Dome, where 175° water pours at 300,000 gallons per minute. The water in the 35-by-90-foot pool is tempered to a swim-friendly 98° to 100°, and there's a kid-sized waterslide and a basketball hoop for playtime. Alongside the pool is a hot tub, with waters kept at 100° to 104°, for steamy soaks. There are changing rooms, hot showers, and concrete decks with chairs for sunning.

Top: Waunita Hot Springs has the hottest natural hot spring water in the state.
Bottom: Alongside the Waunita Hot Springs pool is a hot tub for steamy soaks, with waters kept at 100° to 104°. PHOTOS BY STEWART M. GREEN

The Site

Whether you go for the vacation rental or the bed-and-breakfast, you'll find very comfortable accommodations at Waunita Hot Springs Ranch. There are two big lodges, the Main and Hillside. Each one has rooms of various configurations, with twenty-six bedrooms sleeping about forty people total. The Main Lodge has rooms with single beds, two beds, bunk beds, and adjoining rooms with beds for families, and each of the rooms in this lodge has a private bath. Built in 1920 on the original foundation of a three-story hotel that burned down in 1915, the structure has all the charm of an early twentieth-century ranch house but has been very well maintained by owners Ryan and Tammy Pringle. The Hillside house comprises four two-room units, with six bathrooms total, and the setup is convenient for families who want to share some space yet still have their individual privacy.

Hot Springs History

Dr. Charles Davis from Chicago operated a very successful sanctuary for his patients here in the early 1900s, until his hotel burned to the ground. Five years later another structure was built on the site and now serves as the Main Lodge. Over the years, the site served as a log bathhouse, mining camp, resort, and home of the minor league Monarch Baseball Camp. The property was purchased by Rod and Junelle Pringle in 1962, and is still owned and managed by the Pringle family.

Area Highlights

The San Isabel and Gunnison National Forests are at your doorstep at Waunita Hot Springs Ranch. You'll find miles of trails and wilderness for hiking, biking, mountaineering adventures, snowshoeing, and cross-country skiing. For downhill skiing and snowboarding, Monarch Mountain Ski Area is just east of the ranch, on Monarch Pass.

Located about 16 miles west of the town of Gunnison, three reservoirs are found in the Curecanti National Recreation Area, including Blue Mesa Reservoir, the largest body of water in the state. Boating, swimming, and windsailing are all popular activities here. At the Morrow Point Reservoir, you can take a scenic boat tour into the Black Canyon of the Gunnison. Just keep in mind that access requires making your way down and then back up 232 stairs on the Pine Creek Trail!

For a relaxing drive, check out the West Elk Loop Scenic Byway, a 204-mile loop around the West Elk Mountains northwest of Gunnison that's been described as "the closest you can come to a wilderness experience in a passenger car." This is an excellent route for wildlife viewing, and during the autumn months, it's perfect for watching the aspens turn from green to gold. If you do the whole loop, expect a long drive, up to 8 hours—plus time to stop for picture taking, picnicking, and maybe even a little shopping in Crested Butte.

The local airport has direct flights from Denver through the winter, so access to Monarch Mountain, Crested Butte Mountain Resort, and the ranch is good year-round from just about anywhere. After a long day on the slopes, Waunita Hot Springs Ranch is a warm, soft place to come home to for a hot soak, a hot meal, and a good night's sleep.

21. CONUNDRUM HOT SPRINGS

Type: Wild outdoor public soaking, plus primitive campsite tent camping.

Location: Trailhead located south of Aspen; the hike to the hot spring is about 17 miles round-trip, in the Maroon Bells–Snowmass Wilderness.

When to visit: Mid-July through mid-October, depending on snow and creek conditions.

Access: Year-round access to the trailhead on public roads, but avalanche conditions may exist on trails, and creek crossings may be dangerous during times of snowfall and snow-melt. No ADA access.

Accommodations: Tent camping at 20 designated campsites by permit only; RV parks and motels are 6.5 miles north of the trailhead in Aspen.

Rules: Clothing is optional. Tent camping by permit only through Recreation.gov; dispersed camping is not allowed. White River National Forest and Maroon Bells–Snowmass Wilderness Area regulations apply. Wag bags are required.

Services: Full services in nearby Aspen.

Maps & GPS: *DeLorme: Colorado Atlas & Gazetteer:* p. 46, E3; Maroon Bells and Hayden Peak Quadrangles. Trailhead 39.119400 / -106.856100; hot springs 39.011550 / -106.891333.

Contact: USDA Forest Service, White River National Forest, Aspen-Sopris Ranger District, 806 W. Hallam St., Aspen, CO 81611; (970) 925-3445; www.fs.usda.gov/whiteriver.

How to get there: From Aspen, take East Main Street west to West Main Street and go 0.2 mile, then turn right onto North 7th Street and left onto CO 82 West/West Hallam Street. Drive 0.5 mile to the traffic circle, and take the third exit onto Castle Creek Road. Go 4.9 miles and bear right onto Conundrum Creek Road, then go 0.9 mile to Conundrum Creek Trailhead.

OVERVIEW

Conundrum Hot Springs aren't the largest, the hottest, the deepest, or the cleanest hot spring pools in Colorado. They are by far, however, the most difficult to reach. There are no hot showers, saunas, spas, or snack bars nearby. Instead, should you choose to make the trek to these lukewarm, slightly muddy waters, you'll have to settle for the simple amenities that nature has laid out for you. To the north of the hot springs lies a deep, sprawling valley lush with green pine and white aspen trees and littered with wildflowers of every hue, while to the south, Triangle Pass rises high on the horizon, bordered by 13,000-foot snow-splattered peaks. To the east and west of the hot springs, ragged ridges scrape the sky, rising thousands of feet from the valley floor, the rugged peaks of the Elk Mountain Range. It's a trade-off of luxury for landscape, and service for scenery—and one happily accepted by hundreds of hot springs buffs who make the journey to Conundrum Hot Springs each year.

The Hot Springs

The sizes, depths, and temperatures of Conundrum Hot Springs vary with the seasons and weather events like rain, snow, and spring melt-off. Approaching from the north

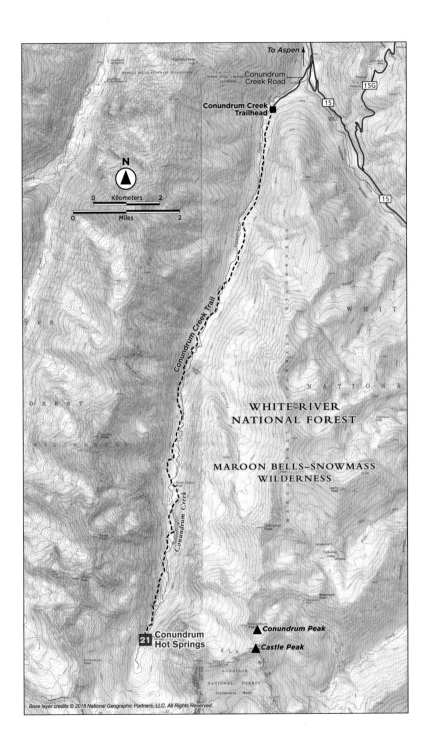

To Aspen

Conundrum
Creek Road

Conundrum Creek
Trailhead

15G

15

N

Kilometers
0   2

Miles
0   2

Conundrum Creek Trail

WHITE

NATIONAL

WHITE-RIVER
NATIONAL FOREST

Conundrum Creek

MAROON BELLS–SNOWMASS
WILDERNESS

21 Conundrum
Hot Springs

Conundrum Peak

Castle Peak

Base layer credits © 2018 National Geographic Partners, LLC. All Rights Reserved.

and traveling uphill, you come to the lower pools first, but continue up to the main pool. This pool is about 25 feet across and 3 feet deep, and it can get muddy when a lot of people are moving about, "stirring the pot." The lower pools vary in size, shape, and clarity, from acceptable for soaking to virtual mud baths. After a soak, rinse off with a cool plunge in Conundrum Creek.

The Site

This is the longest hike in the book to the highest hot springs in Colorado. With the trailhead about 8,700 feet above sea level and the hot springs at about 11,200 feet, you will gain nearly 2,500 feet of elevation and travel almost 9 miles to reach the waters. If you are accustomed to this type of hiking, then you will enjoy a moderate albeit long day hike along a well-worn trail in a beautiful area of Colorado. If you are not, consider breaking the trip up into two or more days to avoid overexertion.

The trail to Conundrum Hot Springs begins at the Conundrum Creek Trailhead and follows Conundrum Creek south for the entire distance to the hot springs. From there, it continues on all the way to Crested Butte, for a total distance of more than 17 miles. Most visitors choose to make this an out-and-back trip to the hot springs only, though.

From the Conundrum Creek Trailhead, the trail starts on the east side of the creek and enters the Maroon Bells–Snowmass Wilderness Area at 0.3 mile. The route here is easy and bordered by meadows and aspen forests, rising ever so gently as it takes you south and deeper into the wilderness. At 2.7 miles the trail crosses a bridge over to the west side of the creek. Although the bridges on this trail are well built and sturdy, each one is simply a long timber sliced in two, set about 10 feet above the rushing waters of Conundrum Creek. There are no handrails, so you will want to watch your step. At about 4.1 miles you will catch your first glimpse of the high dome of Castleabra to the south; this thirteener is close to the hot springs and will give you a good idea of just how far you have left to travel. At about 6 miles there is a second bridge and views of Electric Pass—at 13,494 feet, the highest trail pass in the United States—to the east. This is a good place to filter drinking water, if you need to do so. Cross the bridge to gain the east side of the creek and continue on past Silver Dollar Ponds. The trail turns rockier and rises more steeply from this point on. The third creek crossing is at about 6.5 miles. This area is a mishmash of fallen trees, and there is no bridge, but the creek widens here to a crossable depth. Take off your boots, put on your water shoes, roll up your pants, get out your trekking poles for balance, and find the shallowest route to make your way over to the west side of the creek. There, you will pick up the trail again, and there's a nice big log just ahead where you can sit down and put your boots and socks back on. You may want to rest here and have a snack too; although the hot springs are just over 2 miles ahead, much of the overall elevation is gained in this final stretch. At about 7 miles you will cross a short talus field, and at about 8 miles you'll find the first designated campsites to the left of the trail. At 8.3 miles you'll cross the final bridge, with the hot springs just beyond.

If you plan on making your tour of Conundrum Hot Springs an overnight trip, the soonest you can set up camp is about 0.25 mile from the trailhead, as soon as you

WHITE RIVER NATIONAL FOREST AND MAROON BELLS–SNOWMASS WILDERNESS AREA

Comprising 2.3 million acres, White River National Forest was established in 1891 as the White River Plateau Timber Reserve and transferred to the Forest Service in 1905. Ten 14,000-foot peaks lie within its borders, along with twelve ski resorts and eight wilderness areas. One of the most beautiful—and probably the most visited and photographed—is the Maroon Bells–Snowmass Wilderness Area, home to the Elk Mountain Range and six of the most difficult fourteeners in the state. There are roughly 100 miles of trail through this wilderness area, and nine passes that rise over 12,000 feet, making this a favorite for mountaineers, day hikers, and backpackers alike. Established under the 1964 Wilderness Act, there are regulations in place to keep the area pristine yet accessible to visitors.

Motor vehicles, bicycles, and wheeled modes of transportation of any kind are not allowed in the wilderness. If you want to get to the hot springs, plan on walking. For camping, set up your tent no closer to a water source than 100 feet, and no closer than 0.3 mile to the hot springs, unless you're in a designated campsite. Likewise, campfires are not allowed within 100 feet of a water source or within 0.3 mile of the hot springs. Signs are posted reminding you that a campfire will cost you a fine of several hundred dollars. Dogs are not allowed within Conundrum Creek Valley, from Silver Dollar Ponds (located 2.3 miles north of Conundrum Hot Springs) to Triangle Pass (1.5 miles southwest of the hot springs). In other words, if you plan on visiting Conundrum Hot Springs, leave your pets at home. If you're camping, be sure to reserve a campsite well in advance. Visitors to this area are asked to carry out all solid human waste—in addition to their standard trash—so be sure to grab a "poop bag" at the trailhead for this purpose. In 2011 the Forest Service was providing these at no charge, but you may want to check with the Aspen-Sopris Ranger District ahead of time to see if they are still being made available, or if you'll need to purchase them in town. If you plan on utilizing Conundrum Creek for your drinking water, carry a filter and liter bottles to fill, and avoid using creek water as you approach the hot springs, as both human and canine fecal matter have been found in the water due to overuse of the area, dogs being allowed in the creek, and people camping too close to the water and not carrying out their waste. Instead, filter early (during the first 5 miles of your hike); utilize rivulets outside the creek when they are available; and, once you've reached the hot springs, hike beyond them to filter from water sources at higher ground. When traveling in any wilderness area, it's best to follow the seven Leave No Trace principles:

1. Plan ahead and prepare.
2. Travel and camp on durable surfaces.
3. Dispose of waste properly.
4. Leave what you find.
5. Minimize campfire impacts.
6. Respect wildlife.
7. Be considerate of other visitors.

Details of the principles can be found on the Leave No Trace Center for Outdoor Ethics website (www.lnt.org).

enter the Maroon Bells–Snowmass Wilderness Area. The terrain here is dense with brush, though, so you may want to hike in a bit farther, as there are open meadows just ahead. From there, you will remain in the wilderness area for the rest of the hike and can set up a tent anywhere as long as it's 100 feet from the creek, for sanitary reasons.

There are twenty signed and designated campsites located at the hot springs. These are quite popular—especially on summer weekends—and as of 2018, reservations are required.

It's a good idea to check in with the rangers at the Aspen-Sopris Ranger District before your hike, to see if there are fire bans or other temporary restrictions in effect in the Maroon Bells–Snowmass Wilderness Area, and to get the latest report on Conundrum Creek Trail conditions.

Area Highlights

As tempting as Conundrum Hot Springs may be on a cold day, the hike in can be dangerous in winter and spring. Avalanches tumbling down from surrounding high peaks bury the trail, and melting snow can make the creek crossings extremely hazardous. This is unfortunate, for a trip to this area could easily be combined with side trips to the many ski resorts in the Aspen area.

There's no reason to fret, though; Aspen is surrounded by plenty of summertime activities to supplement your Conundrum Hot Springs adventure. If you're staying in the Maroon Bells–Snowmass Wilderness Area, you can extend your visit with a longer hike to Crested Butte, or take advantage of many other trails that weave through the Elk Mountain Range, over high passes and across wildflower-strewn valleys. Or head to Maroon Lake for views of the most-photographed site in the state, the famous (and infamous) Maroon Bells—also known as "The Deadly Bells"— two pyramid-shaped peaks that have taken the lives of many skilled but unfortunate mountaineers. The views from the lake are simply stunning, and from here you can hike the 1.3-mile Maroon Lake Scenic Loop or opt for the 4.5-mile round-trip hike to Crater Lake.

For more adventure, head northwest into the Roaring Fork Valley for whitewater rafting on the Roaring Fork River. If you prefer to enjoy the beauty of Pitkin County from the front seat of your car, drive over Independence Pass on CO 82, between Aspen and Leadville. Straddling the Continental Divide at its 12,095-foot high point, Independence Pass is the highest paved mountain pass in Colorado.

Facing page: Despite the long hike, Conundrum Hot Springs attracts soakers seven days a week from July through October. SUSAN JOY PAUL

22. PENNY HOT SPRINGS

Type: Wild outdoor public soaking.

Location: Pitkin County north of Redstone, with parking located at a pullout on the east side of CO 133 about 13 miles south of Carbondale, and the hot springs located about 50 feet below the road, on Crystal River.

When to visit: 7 days a week year-round.

Access: Year-round vehicle access on public roads. No ADA access.

Accommodations: None on-site, but lodging is available 1 mile north at Avalanche Ranch Hot Springs, and tent and RV camping and motels are located 4 miles south in Redstone and 13 miles north in Carbondale.

Rules: Clothing is recommended. Even though this is a wild spring, it's located in a public open space, and soakers are in view of people at the pullout. No camping within 0.25 mile of Crystal River. Follow Leave No Trace principles (https://lnt.org) and Pitkin County Open Space regulations (http://pitkincounty.com/772/Properties-Trails).

Services: Services 4 miles south in Redstone and 13 miles north in Carbondale.

Maps & GPS: *DeLorme: Colorado Atlas & Gazetteer:* p. 45, C8; *National Geographic Trails Illustrated #128,* Maroon Bells, Redstone, Marble; Redstone Quadrangle. Parking 39.231934 / -107.227488; hot springs 39.231812 / -107.227263.

Contact: Pitkin County, Basalt, CO 81621; (970) 920-5200; http://pitkincounty.com.

How to get there: From Carbondale, take CO 133 South for 11.8 miles to a pullout on the left side of the road. If you're coming from the south on CO 133 through Redstone, the hot springs are about 5 miles past Hayes Creek Falls and just past mile marker 55, on the right. Park in the large pullout lot and descend to the west side of the Crystal River.

OVERVIEW

This roadside hot spring, located within Penny Hot Springs Open Space, is popular with locals and passersby year-round.

The Hot Springs

The size, depth, temperature, and condition of Penny Hot Springs vary with the seasons, but you will usually find three or more soaking pools here. In the spring of 2017, the largest one was about 15 feet in diameter and a couple of feet deep, but locals say it's often twice that size. Temperatures range from about 90° at the source to much cooler around the perimeter, where Crystal River waters seep in.

The Site

Even though Penny Hot Springs is so close to the highway, it's situated along the river with beautiful views all around. The granite cliffs of Hells Gate line the Crystal River Valley, and the Elk Range's Mount Sopris is visible to the northeast. Plan a weekday visit to increase your chances of having the springs to yourself.

Penny Hot Springs is popular with locals and passersby year-round.
STEWART M. GREEN

Top: Penny Hot Springs is just off the highway, four miles north of Redstone.
Bottom: Soakers enjoy the wild pool at Penny Hot Springs. PHOTOS BY STEWART M. GREEN

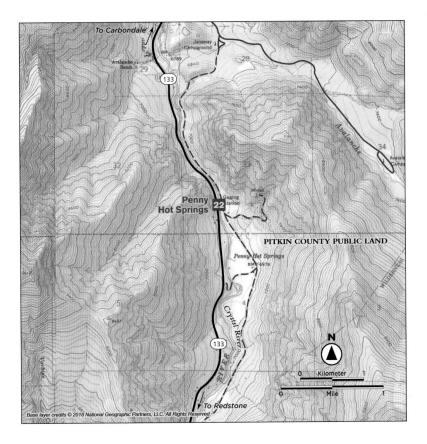

Area Highlights

Penny Hot Springs is located on the West Elk Loop Scenic Byway, 204 miles of drivable Colorado splendor that wraps around the West Elk Mountains from Gunnison to Crested Butte and Crawford to Paonia, then stretches north from McClure Pass to Carbondale. The last section of byway is known as the Ruby Route, and passes through Redstone, a scenic, historic town with plenty of outdoor adventure, including rock climbing at Redstone Boulders and ice climbing at Redstone Pillar and Hayes Creek Falls. In the summertime, hike the East Creek Trail for views of the town, and in winter enjoy ice skating at Redstone Park Pond. Tour the newly rehabilitated, historic Redstone Castle anytime. Amid all that activity, pause on your trip for a toasty dip at Penny Hot Springs.

23. AVALANCHE RANCH CABINS & HOT SPRINGS

Type: Family-oriented outdoor public swimming and soaking with quiet hours, plus lodging.

Location: Redstone, about 25 miles south of Glenwood Springs.

When to visit: Open year-round, but pools are closed during the day on Wednesday for cleaning and reopen in the evening for lodging guests only.

Access: Year-round vehicle access on public roads. Call ahead for ADA access details.

Accommodations: 14 private cabins, 3 covered wagons, loft above the gift shop, 1 tiny house, and a 3-bedroom ranch house that sleeps 8.

Rules: Day-soakers welcome, except Wednesday when the pools are closed during the day. Clothing is required. No smoking. No glass and no pets in pool area. Pets allowed in lodgings with fee.

Services: Limited services 4 miles south in Redstone and 12 miles north in Carbondale. Limited cell service and Wi-Fi.

Map & GPS: *DeLorme: Colorado Atlas & Gazetteer:* p. 45, C8; 39.247347 / -107.237824.

Contact: Avalanche Ranch Cabins & Hot Springs, 12863 CO 133, Redstone, CO 81623; (970) 963-2846; http:// avalancheranch.com. Call or visit website for rates, reservations, and hours of operation.

How to get there: From Carbondale, take CO 133 South for 10.6 miles and turn right into Avalanche Ranch Cabins & Hot Springs.

OVERVIEW

Avalanche Ranch Cabins & Hot Springs sits on the hillside above the West Elk Loop Scenic Byway, nestled in the woods and away from traffic. This quiet little getaway seems secluded but isn't far from town.

The Hot Springs

Hot spring water pours from a rustic cabin at 104° and cascades through three pools with temps ranging from 95° to 105°. The lowest, coolest pool is also the biggest, at 15 feet by 30 feet, and attracts young swimmers. The middle pool, the hottest, is 15 feet by 20 feet, and the highest pool is 15 feet by 10 feet; both are soaking pools with quiet, relaxed atmospheres. Decks surround the pools, with views of Mount Sopris to the east. The water comes from two wells located on the property that are 100° and 109°. The hot springs pools refresh completely every 2 hours, and guests have 24-hour access.

The Site

Avalanche Hot Springs is a 36-acre ranch and working farm located north of Penny Hot Springs, on the west side of the road. Most of the private cabins have full kitchens, and all have private bathrooms, while the tiny house has a minifridge, microwave, and separate bath, and the wagons each have a coffee pot and share a communal shower

Top: The swimming pool at Avalanche Ranch Cabins & Hot Springs is a great choice for the kids.
Bottom: Mount Sopris provides a stunning backdrop at Avalanche Ranch Cabins & Hot Springs.
PHOTOS BY STEWART M. GREEN

Hot springs water pours from a cabin and feeds the pools at Avalanche Ranch Hot Springs.
STEWART M. GREEN

and bathroom. The barn is a multipurpose area, used for massage, yoga, and retreats, and the cabins have charcoal grills. There's plenty to do on the property, with access to hiking trails, ponds and the river for boating, plus volleyball, horseshoes, and yoga. In the winter, go sledding, snowshoeing, and ice skating. You can also browse the gift and antiques shop, or hang out in the lodge, which is open to guests 24 hours a day. Massage services are available with 48-hour notice.

Commercial hot springs sometimes offer sleeping options such as this covered wagon at Avalanche Ranch Cabins & Hot Springs. STEWART M. GREEN

Avalanche Ranch is a beautifully scenic spot for weddings and other events, and is also available for meetings and retreats. Lodging is available for up to seventy-five people.

Hot Springs History
The Ogilvy family has owned next-door Hell Roaring Ranch since 1978 but did not drill for hot water until 2008, when melting snow caused by hot air rising from the ground was observed along the west side of the highway. Later that year, two wells were drilled, and in 2010 a pipe was laid and construction began on the hot springs pools. The property is still owned and operated by the Ogilvy family.

Area Highlights
Avalanche Ranch Cabins & Hot Springs is a lovely place to relax or enjoy on-site recreation, but if you want to wander up the road, Carbondale is just a few miles north. There's shopping, restaurants, and live theater at Thunder River Theatre Company. Enjoy whitewater rafting and kayaking on Roaring Fork and Crystal Rivers and cross-country skiing on the Spring Gulch Nordic Trail System. Outfitters are available, and afterward you can ease your weary muscles with a soak and a swim at Avalanche Hot Springs.

24. GLENWOOD HOT SPRINGS RESORT

Type: Family-oriented, resort-style outdoor public swimming and soaking, plus massage and spa services, lodging, and fitness center.

Location: Glenwood Springs, about 160 miles west of Denver and 87 miles east of Grand Junction.

When to visit: 7 days a week year-round.

Access: Year-round vehicle access on public roads. Call ahead for ADA access details.

Accommodations: 107-room lodge.

Rules: Day-soakers welcome. Clothing is required. No smoking in the lodge, at the pool, or any other public area. No alcohol allowed at the pool. No tents, umbrellas, or other shade structures allowed. No pets except for guide animals.

Services: Full services in Glenwood Springs.

Map & GPS: *DeLorme: Colorado Atlas & Gazetteer:* p. 35, E7; 39.549627 / -107.323489.

Contact: Glenwood Hot Springs Resort, 401 N. River St., Glenwood Springs, CO 81601; (970) 947-2955; www.hotspringspool.com. Call or visit website for rates, reservations, and hours of operation.

How to get there: In Glenwood Springs, take CO 82 East and turn right onto 6th Street. Go 0.2 mile and turn right onto North River Street. Continue 0.1 mile to Glenwood Hot Springs, on the right.

OVERVIEW

Glenwood Hot Springs is an expansive soaking and swimming destination that, due to its sheer size, might be mistaken for a Rhode Island beach. The centerpiece is an enormous swimming pool—at 405 feet long by 100 feet wide, it's the largest hot spring pool on the planet. Located just off the highway in Glenwood Springs, this hot springs resort is practically a small city in its own right, boasting pools, cabanas, waterslides, a large athletic club, full-service spa, restaurant, snack bar, sport shop, and a 107-room lodge. And when you stand at one end of the pool and try to find the other end, well, don't. You'll just give yourself a headache and spoil all the fun!

The Hot Springs

The big pool is roughly the size of a football field and contains more than a million gallons of water. Cool water brings the temperature to about 90°, just right for swimming laps and water play. The west end of the pool is 12 feet deep and has two diving boards, plus several lap lanes. The outdoor pools are surrounded by concrete decks, cabanas, and lounge chairs. There are two big slides too: The Green Amazon is an inner-tube slide, and the Blue Comet is a body slide, and they both dump you into a shallow pool outside of the swimming and soaking pools. The swimming pool has eight coin-operated "bubble chairs" situated along the edges that will give you an invigorating 5-minute hydromassage, so be sure to bring some quarters. The smaller pool at Glenwood Hot Springs, known as the Therapy or Kiddie Pool, is 100 feet long and 2 feet deep and contains nearly 100,000 gallons of water. The temperature is

Top: Night settles in over the big hot springs pool at Glenwood Hot Springs Resort.
Bottom: The world's biggest outdoor hot spring pool is at Glenwood Hot Springs Resort.
PHOTOS COURTESY GLENWOOD HOT SPRINGS

Kayakers practice their moves at Glenwood Hot Springs Resort. STEWART M. GREEN

maintained at about 104°, and the underwater benches and stairs make it a comfy place for a hot soak. The pools are fed by the Yampah Spring, which produces more than 3.5 million gallons of 122° water every day, enough to completely replenish the Kiddie Pool every 2 hours and the swimming pool every 6 hours.

The water is filtered with an ozone purification system, and chlorine is added. The hot spring water is also used to heat the lodge and spa, making it the largest geothermally heated building in Colorado. Finally, the changing area at Glenwood Hot Springs has a few family dressing rooms, making it easier for moms and dads to get the little ones in and out of their suits with plenty of room to spread out.

The Site

There's plenty to do in and out of the water at Glenwood Hot Springs. Five mesh-enclosed cabanas—available for rent by the day or the half day—offer a degree of privacy for group events. Some are high up on raised decks, and two lower ones are close together and poolside, making them a popular spot for kids' birthday parties. Call well ahead to reserve the cabanas, especially in the summertime, when they're in high demand. A miniature golf course located near the waterslides is well shaded by trees, which also serve to filter out the pool noise. The kids can enjoy a shaved ice afterward and maybe get a temporary tattoo. Other amenities include the Grill restaurant, a poolside snack bar, and picnic areas where you can enjoy your meal. Be sure to grab some popcorn and soft-serve ice cream for dessert!

Once you've had enough sunshine, head indoors to the Athletic Club. For a daily rate, you can take advantage of the "wet lounge" for indoor soaking and steaming. There's a big Jacuzzi tub, steam room, and a dry sauna. The fitness center here has lots of classes, including Pilates and Spin, or you can go it alone with cardio machines, weight machines, or free weights, or sweat it out on the racquetball or handball courts. The adjoining Spa of the Rockies is a luxurious full-service spa and salon where you can get rubbed, scrubbed, tanned, toned, soaked, polished, wrapped, waxed, kneaded, clipped, purified, and revitalized into delirious oblivion.

If you'd like to stay the night, there's a beautiful, newly remodeled 107-room lodge just north of the pool. The building itself is quite pretty, and like the rest of the grounds at Glenwood Springs, it's lush with greenery. Virginia creeper hangs about the brickwork, and the sweet smell of pink and white lilacs fills the air. From here, you're within walking distance of downtown Glenwood Springs for shopping, restaurants, and nighttime entertainment.

Hot Springs History

Richard Sopris was the first white man to visit the hot springs, and in 1860 he named the place Grand Springs. In 1883, prospectors renamed it Defiance, and in 1885, Isaac Cooper from Iowa purchased 400 acres for a township, which he renamed Glenwood Springs. In 1887 the land was deeded to Walter Devereaux, who had learned about the springs from mountain man Kit Carson. Devereaux developed the caves at nearby Yampah Vapor Caves and began work on the big swimming pool at Glenwood Springs. The Hot Springs Pool was completed in 1888, and after passing through several owners, the property and business were sold in 1956 for $1,000,000.

Area Highlights

You could spend the whole day or longer at Glenwood Hot Springs and not get bored, but if you want to get away from it all for a while, grab your rock-climbing gear and head to Grizzly Creek, No Name Canyon, Puoux and Super Puoux, Rifle Mountain Park, Shoshone and Stones, and, of course, Glenwood Canyon. Guide services aplenty can get you started, if you're new to the sport. There are ropes courses and zip-line tours available, too, plus lots of scenery to enjoy while you're navigating the greenery. In the wintertime enjoy ice skating at the Glenwood Springs Community Center, or skiing and snowboarding at Sunlight Mountain Resort. If you want to travel a bit, there are half a dozen world-class ski resorts within an hour's drive of Glenwood Springs, including Aspen, Vail, Beaver Creek, and Snowmass. Glenwood Springs may seem like the perfect place to spend some time, or maybe even live, and that's a common sentiment among all those who visit. Beyond all the activities and the hot springs, it's a gorgeous area surrounded by national forestland, high cliffs, and higher peaks, with rivers rushing through and more scenery than you can take in during a single visit.

25. YAMPAH SPA & SALON: THE HOT SPRINGS VAPOR CAVES

Type: Cozy, quiet, indoor private soaking and public vapor caves, plus massage and spa services.

Location: Glenwood Springs, about 160 miles west of Denver and 87 miles east of Grand Junction.

When to visit: 7 days a week year-round.

Access: Year-round vehicle access on public roads. Call ahead for ADA access details.

Accommodations: None on-site, but tent and RV camping and motels are located in Glenwood Springs.

Rules: Day-soaker facility. Clothing is required in the caves, but optional in the private baths. No smoking, no alcohol, and no pets.

Services: Full services in Glenwood Springs.

Map & GPS: *DeLorme: Colorado Atlas & Gazetteer:* p. 35, E7; 39.550657 / -107.320188.

Contact: Yampah Spa & Salon, 709 6th St., Glenwood Springs, CO 81601; (970) 945-0667; www.yampahspa .com. Call or visit website for rates and hours of operation.

How to get there: In Glenwood Springs, take CO 82 East and turn right onto 6th Street. Go 0.2 mile and turn left onto East 6th Street and Yampah Hot Springs Vapor Caves, on the left.

OVERVIEW

Yampah Hot Springs houses the only natural vapor caves known to exist in North America, and they're the star attraction at this full-service spa and salon. Relax in the underground caves, soak in a private tub of hot mineral water, and enjoy some cooling-off time in the solarium. Yampah Hot Springs is a cozy, quiet, one-stop shop for a steam, soak, nap, wrap, scrub, rub, mani, pedi, massage, masque, and more.

The Hot Springs

Yampah Hot Springs is tucked against the hillside like a pretty pink cupcake stuffed with sweet promises of refreshment, beauty, and rebirth. But underneath that fluffy icing lies the real attraction: underground caves where 125° hot spring water flows freely along the floors, filling the air with a 115° mineral mist and enveloping guests in a penetrating steam bath. Don your swimsuit and waterproof sandals, grab a towel for your head, and relax on century-old marble benches in three chambers plus a cooling area.

For soaking, reserve a Japanese-style mineral bath filled with natural spring water. The mineral water is hot and lightly sulfurous, and you can adjust the temperature with cold water from a second tap. The baths here are clothing-optional and very popular, especially for couples. Fresh flowers, candlelight, gentle music, and cool cups of citrus water conspire to soothe your every sense and inspire sultry visions.

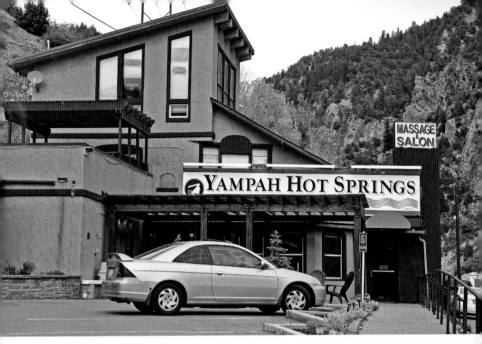

Top: Yampah Spa & Salon: The Hot Springs Vapor Caves is a cozy, quiet, one-stop shop for a steam, soak, nap, wrap, scrub, rub, mani, pedi, massage, masque, and more. Bottom: The Hot Springs Vapor Caves houses the only natural vapor caves known to exist in North America. PHOTOS BY STEWART M. GREEN

The Site

After your steam or soak, cool down in the solarium. The comfy lounge chairs, natural lighting and moderate temperature make this a good place to read a book or simply doze off for a while. Book a private massage, body wrap, scrub, or therapy, or head upstairs to Aveda Salon for hair, skin, and nail treatments. This is a great place to indulge yourself for a couple's getaway or simply some quiet, luxurious "me" time.

Hot Springs History

Prior to 1860, Ute Indians enjoyed the hot springs and vapor caves of Glenwood Springs and called the waters *yampah*, or "big medicine." James Landis from Leadville claimed the hot springs, and after many subsequent sales and development, the Yampah vapor caves were purchased by the current owner, Patsy Steele, who overhauled the facility in 1990.

Although there were originally three separate vapor caves, the three-chambered vapor cave at Yampah is the only one known to have been put to commercial use. Another one was sealed during construction by the Denver & Rio Grande Railroad, and the track there is still in use as part of the Southern Pacific Railroad. The location of the third vapor cave remains a mystery to all, save for the ghosts of Utes who basked and bathed there more than a hundred years ago, and residents of Glenwood Springs who prefer to keep this sacred place a local secret.

Area Highlights

Situated on the confluence of the Colorado and Roaring Fork Rivers, there's plenty to do in Glenwood Springs. Kayaking, canoeing, rafting, and stand-up paddleboarding are popular activities, or head to White River National Forest—the largest national forest in Colorado—for hiking, biking, snowshoeing, and camping.

The Rio Grande Trail offers a paved, 41-mile route from Glenwood Springs to Aspen and is popular with bicyclists and inline skaters. You can turn around at any point or choose a shorter trail, like the River Trail, which follows the Roaring Fork River. Book a paragliding, motorcycle, or Segway trip in the summer, and enjoy skiing, snowshoeing, and snowboarding at Sunlight Mountain Resort in winter. There are plenty of ways to wear yourself weary in Glenwood Springs, and a hot soak and a steam waiting to refresh you back at Yampah Spa.

26. IRON MOUNTAIN HOT SPRINGS

Type: Family-oriented outdoor public swimming and soaking with quiet area.

Location: Glenwood Springs, about 160 miles west of Denver and 87 miles east of Grand Junction.

When to visit: 7 days a week year-round, except Christmas, Thanksgiving, and 4 days in July for cleaning.

Access: Year-round vehicle access on public roads. There's ADA access to all upper mineral pools and a wheelchair ramp to the swimming pool. ADA shower and aqua chair.

Accommodations: None on-site, but tent and RV camping and motels are located in Glenwood Springs.

Rules: Day-soaker facility. Clothing is required. No smoking, no drugs, no alcohol, no glass, and no pets allowed.

Services: Full services in Glenwood Springs.

Map & GPS: *DeLorme: Colorado Atlas & Gazetteer:* p. 35, E7; 39.555213 / -107.336471.

Contact: Iron Mountain Hot Springs, 281 Centennial St., Glenwood Springs, CO 81601; (970) 945-4766; www.iron mountainhotsprings.com. Call or visit website for rates and hours of operation.

How to get there: In Glenwood Springs, take CO 82 East and turn left onto West 6th Street. Go 0.3 mile and turn left onto Devereux Road. Continue 0.3 mile and turn right onto Centennial Street, then go 0.2 mile to Iron Mountain Hot Springs.

OVERVIEW

The Colorado River and Rocky Mountains provide a lovely backdrop to Glenwood Springs' newest soaking spot, a sunny site that's well-suited for families, couples, and anyone who wants a soak with a view.

The Hot Springs

Sixteen individual soaking pools, a freshwater swimming pool, and a jetted spa pool offer plenty of options for every kind of soaker.

The hot mineral soaking pools are a designated quiet zone. Each pool is signed, and the daily water temperatures are posted in the lobby. Two of them are reflexology pools.

The waters that fill the soaking pools are sourced from three hot springs: Redstone, Gamba, and Hobo. The water, flowing at 170 gallons per minute, ranges from 92° to 120° and is combined, then run alongside cold water in a cooling tower, adjusting it to comfortable soaking temperatures of 98° to 108°. The pools have continuous flow and completely replenish every 2 hours. No chemicals are added to the water. Children under 5 are not allowed in the soaking pools.

Kids of all ages can enjoy the big 93° Family Pool and the adjoining 103° jetted spa. The water in these pools is not hot spring water but geothermally heated. They're set away from the soaking pools, so the kids can have fun without disturbing soakers.

Top: Two reflexology pools are featured at Iron Mountain Hot Springs. Bottom: The big family pool is the place for kids at Iron Mountain Hot Springs. PHOTOS BY STEWART M. GREEN

The Site

Iron Mountain has a large bathhouse and lockers, and a gift shop with apparel and souvenirs. The Sopris Café sells wraps, salad, pizza, and more, and there's a snack bar for light food and drinks. Between soaks, the covered patio is the perfect place to cool off in summer or warm up in winter. Beer, wine, and premixed cocktails are also available.

Seasonally in the evening, you can enjoy "Rhythm on the River," light music provided by local bands.

Hot Springs History

Dating back to the 1800s, numerous iterations of commercial soaking sites preceded Iron Mountain. The West Glenwood Health Spa, Wash Allen Bathhouse, Gamba Mineral Springs, Glenwood Health Spa, and Fort Defiance Bathhouse all operated here, and the final structure was torn down in 1996. After languishing for many years, the site was brought back to life when current owners Steve and Jeanne Beckley and Mogli and Coop Cooper broke ground at Iron Mountain

Choose from sixteen soaking pools at Iron Mountain Hot Springs. STEWART M. GREEN

in October 2014. The site opened to the public in July 2015.

Area Highlights

Iron Mountain Hot Springs is owned by the same folks who own the Glenwood Caverns Adventure Park & Historic Fairy Caves, so if you're traveling to both, call ahead to inquire about package deals. Glenwood Caverns Adventure Park offers underground walking and spelunking tours of an enormous cave system deep within Iron Mountain. In addition to the caves, this is a veritable amusement park of rides and activities, from the 4,300-foot-long gondola tram that takes you to the caves, to the Giant Canyon Swing that moves in wide arcs 1,300 feet above the Colorado River. After all that excitement, wind down with a quiet soak at Iron Mountain Hot Springs.

27. **SOUTH CANYON HOT SPRINGS**

Type: Wild outdoor public soaking.

Location: Garfield County west of Glenwood Springs, with parking located at a pullout on the west side of South Canyon Creek Road south of I-70, about 6 miles west of Glenwood Springs; the hot springs are located on a hillside about 300 feet away.

When to visit: 7 days a week year-round.

Access: Year-round vehicle access on public roads. No ADA access.

Accommodations: None on-site, but tent and RV camping and motels are located 6 miles east in Glenwood Springs and 8 miles west in New Castle.

Rules: Clothing is optional.

Services: Full services in Glenwood Springs.

Maps & GPS: *DeLorme: Colorado Atlas & Gazetteer*: p. 35, E7; Storm King Mountain Quadrangle. Trailhead 39.554302 / -107.410225; hot springs 39.553650 / -107.410800.

Contact: Garfield County Public Lands Access, 108 8th St., Glenwood Springs, CO 81601; (970) 945-1377 ext. 1730; www.garfield-county.com/public-lands-access/index.aspx.

How to get there: From Glenwood Springs, take I-70 West for 4.8 miles to exit 111 toward South Canyon. Go 0.2 mile and turn left onto CO 134. Drive 1 mile to a pullout on the right side of the road and the start of the trail to South Canyon Hot Springs.

OVERVIEW

Two small undeveloped hot pots make up South Canyon Hot Springs.

South Canyon Hot Springs is a wild spring west of Glenwood Springs. STEWART M. GREEN

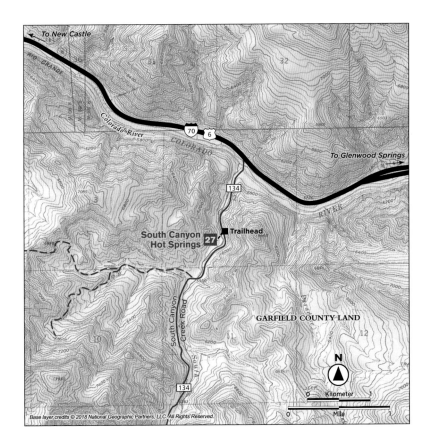

The Hot Springs

A hot spring sprouts from the ground on a roadside hill, carving out craterlike depressions in the earth. Rocks and mud line the bottom of the soaking ponds, and algae is common and may be prevalent. The exact widths, depths, clarity, and temperature of each pot vary on any given day, due to rain, snowmelt, and weather conditions. Occasional caretakers dig out the pools and shore up the sides with rocks.

The Site

The hike to the hot springs is about 0.1 mile round-trip. From the roadside turnout, follow a well-worn path down to a creek and make your way across a wooden board. Hike up a short rise to the hot spring pools. The hot springs are located on county land and not far from a landfill, but views of the surrounding low peaks and meadows make this a lovely spot for a skinny-dip that's outdoors, easily accessible, and free.

Area Highlights

A visit to South Canyon Hot Springs is a good opportunity to visit the Storm King Mountain Memorial Trail, the site of the tragic South Canyon fire that took the lives of fourteen firefighters in 1994. The trail honors these men and women.

The author enjoys a solo soak at South Canyon Hot Springs. STEWART M. GREEN

The trailhead is located 7 miles west of Glenwood Springs on I-70, at Canyon Creek exit 109. Take a right onto the frontage road and head east for a mile to a parking lot at the trailhead.

The trail has been improved by government land management and forest service organizations, as well as volunteers, and there are informational placards along the trail, as well as a Hotshot and Smokejumper Memorial Site and a Helitack Memorial Site.

The wild and rugged terrain of the higher portions of trail remain untouched as a reminder to all of the difficult and challenging conditions faced by firefighters who struggle in the battle to control Colorado wildfires. It is a fitting tribute to those brave men and women who perished on Storm King Mountain.

NORTHERN ROCKIES COLORADO HOT SPRINGS

STEAMBOAT SPRINGS

Year-round hot spring splendor awaits in northern Colorado with swimming pools and soaking ponds, a walking tour through Steamboat Springs, and unique overnight accommodations like covered wagons and a train caboose. These hot springs are located within a 3-hour drive from metro Denver and a 4-hour drive from Colorado Springs.

Before or after your soak, enjoy a massage in the hut at Strawberry Park Hot Springs.
STEWART M. GREEN

28. STRAWBERRY PARK HOT SPRINGS

Type: Family-oriented outdoor public swimming and soaking, plus massage services and lodging.

Location: Steamboat Springs, about 160 miles northwest of Denver and 40 miles east of Craig.

When to visit: 7 days a week year-round.

Access: Year-round vehicle access on public roads up to the final 2 miles, where the road is unpaved and steep in places but navigable in a passenger car during the summer. From November 1 to May 1, only 4x4 vehicles with snow tires or any vehicle with chains are permitted on this section, but you can hire a shuttle from one of several operators in Steamboat Springs. Leave RVs behind, as there is nowhere to park them.

Accommodations: 6 cabins and a train caboose available year-round; 2 covered wagons and 5 camping spots open in the summer. More camping nearby, and motels and RV parks are about 7 miles south in Steamboat Springs.

Rules: Day-soakers welcome. Clothing is required during daylight hours but optional after dark. No one under the age of 18 allowed after dark. No smoking, no alcohol, no glass containers, and no pets. **Pay by cash or check—credit cards not accepted.**

Services: No services on-site, and no cell service or Wi-Fi. Full services 7 miles south in Steamboat Springs.

Map & GPS: *DeLorme: Colorado Atlas & Gazetteer:* p. 16, E3; 40.559571 / -106.849578.

Contact: Strawberry Park Hot Springs, 44200 CR 36, Steamboat Springs, CO 80487; (970) 879-0342; http://strawberryhotsprings.com. Call or visit website for rates, reservations, and hours of operation.

How to get there: From Denver, take I-70 West for about 55 miles to exit 205, then turn onto CO 9 West at Silverthorne. Follow CO 9 for about 38 miles to US 40 West and go about 51 miles to Steamboat Springs. Go north on 7th Street and turn right onto Missouri Avenue. Go 0.3 mile on Missouri Avenue, which becomes North Park Road. Turn right onto Strawberry Park Road and drive 0.8 mile, then turn left onto CR 36 and continue 5.1 miles to Strawberry Park Hot Springs.

OVERVIEW

The development at Strawberry Park Hot Springs allows for safe, sustainable access while maintaining the integrity of the natural elements, and the end result is nothing short of exquisite. Hot mineral pools crafted from native stone sidle up alongside the rushing waters of Hot Springs Creek, sprinkled by waterfalls and surrounded by pure, unsullied Colorado backcountry. Dense wood and lush greenery line the banks in the summertime, while winter borders the creek in billowing mounds of fluffy white champagne powder.

Facing page: You can always find a quiet spot for a solo soak at Strawberry Park Hot Springs.
STEWART M. GREEN

The Hot Springs

Underground hot springs bubble up from the bottoms of six outdoor pools—the Main Pool, Bridge Pool, Lower Pool, and several therapy pools—at Strawberry Park Hot Springs. Water temperatures vary from 102° to 105°. No chemicals are added to the water.

The hot springs attract families, couples, and singles of all ages during daylight hours, but after dark they're for adults only and clothing-optional, and the lighting is subdued. If you visit the park at night, leave the kids at home and pack a towel, some water in a non-glass container, and a headlamp or flashlight to light your way to the pools.

The Site

The development here is impressive in its masonry and woodwork, with concrete decks edged in river rock, stone and split-log seating, fire pits, and a coed changing cabin. Massage therapy is available poolside, in huts, on a chair, or even floating on a pool. You can rent towels and suits, and buy water and other non-glass-bottled drinks. Food is not allowed in the pool area, but pack a lunch for the picnic area, and be sure to use a hard cooler to keep out the wild critters. Shaved ice is available seasonally, so bring a few extra dollars.

For lodging, there are six cabins available year-round. Tucked into the hillside above the creek, they're heated and have gas lanterns and grills, but no bedding, running water, or electricity, so plan ahead. Cabin guests share a communal bathhouse with hot showers and toilets, but bring your own towels. There's also a red train caboose with a full kitchen, fireplace, and private bathroom, but it's quite popular, so make reservations well in advance.

In the summer months, Strawberry Park Hot Springs rents out two covered wagons and five tent sites; there is no heat and no lighting, and cooking and candles are not allowed in the wagons. Bring a battery-powered lamp and a camp stove for outdoor cooking, a flashlight or headlamp for getting around at night, and whatever food and water you'll need.

Strawberry Park Hot Springs lies on private property, but an easement provides access to Hot Spring Creek Trail. However, if you park at Strawberry Park, you'll be charged for a day of soaking, so hikers and bikers should park lower down on the road, at the Mad Creek Trailhead or Lower Bear Lake Trailhead. Driving to the hot springs, watch for hikers and bikers along the road, and be respectful of private residents along CR 36, especially during the evening and nighttime hours.

Hot Springs History

The 40 acres at Strawberry Park were homesteaded in the 1880s, and after passing through a number of owners, the property was sold to the City of Steamboat Springs in the early 1930s. The area became increasingly popular and unmanageable, so they put the site on the market. In 1981 the current owner, Don Johnson, purchased the property and began commercial operation. Initially, locals feared their favorite soaking spot would be turned into a theme park, but Johnson won them over with a thoughtful, gentle approach to the development. The pools, changing areas, and bathrooms

Top: Hot mineral pools crafted from native stone sidle up alongside the rushing waters of Hot Springs Creek, sprinkled by waterfalls and surrounded by pure, unsullied Colorado backcountry at Strawberry Park Hot Springs. Bottom: If you visit the park at night, leave the kids at home and pack a towel, some water in a non-glass container, and a headlamp or flashlight to light your way to the pools. PHOTOS BY STEWART M. GREEN

Strawberry Park Hot Springs attracts families, couples, and singles of all ages during daylight hours, but after dark they're for adults only and clothing-optional, and the lighting is subdued.
STEWART M. GREEN

were added, and the current minimalist nature of Strawberry Park Hot Springs strikes a fine balance between a natural setting and welcome amenities and access.

Area Highlights

There are plenty of ways to enjoy Steamboat Springs. With skiing at the Steamboat Ski Resort; kayaking, canoeing, tubing, or rafting the Yampa River; sailing in Stagecoach Reservoir, Lake Catamount, or Steamboat Lake; camping and hiking in the Mount Zirkel and Flat Tops Wilderness Areas; rock climbing and ice climbing at Rabbit Ears Pass and Fish Creek Falls; plus mountain biking and roller-skating, your greatest challenge won't be finding something to do but trying to fit it all in.

The people of Steamboat Springs use any excuse to get outside and revel in the streets with festivals celebrating every occasion. January kicks off the year with MusicFest, February brings the Winter Carnival, and in March, it's the Mardi Gras Festival. Enjoy the Yampa River Festival in May and the Steamboat Marathon in June. In July, there's the Strings Music Fest, the Hot Air Balloon Rodeo, and the Tour de Steamboat Bike Ride, and in August it's time for the Steamboat Wine Festival and Steamboat All Arts Festival. In September, check out OktoberWest, the Steamboat Springs Stage Race, and the Run Rabbit Run 50 Mile Ultra Marathon. This is a mere fraction of the events that go on in this town—the people of Steamboat Springs really know how to be festive! Grab your towel, your bike, your balloon, your kayak, and your skis. A road trip to Steamboat Springs for a hot soak at Strawberry Park could end up just about anywhere.

29. OLD TOWN HOT SPRINGS

Type: Family-oriented outdoor public swimming and soaking, saunas, plus fitness center.

Location: Steamboat Springs, about 160 miles northwest of Denver and 40 miles east of Craig.

When to visit: 7 days a week year-round.

Access: Year-round vehicle access on public roads. Call ahead for ADA access details.

Accommodations: None on-site, but tent and RV camping and motels are located in Steamboat Springs.

Rules: Day-soaker facility. Clothing is required. No smoking, no alcohol, no glass containers, and no pets allowed.

Services: Full services in Steamboat Springs.

Map & GPS: *DeLorme: Colorado Atlas & Gazetteer*: p. 26, A3; 40.482116 / -106.827589.

Contact: Old Town Hot Springs, 136 Lincoln Ave., Steamboat Springs, CO 80487; (970) 879-1828; www.oldtown hotsprings.org. Call or visit website for rates and hours of operation.

How to get there: From Denver, take I-70 West for about 55 miles to exit 205, then turn onto CO 9 West at Silverthorne. Follow CO 9 for about 38 miles to US 40 West and go about 51 miles to Steamboat Springs. Old Town Hot Springs is easily visible on the right side of the road as you get into town.

OVERVIEW

Hot springs can be a solitary affair, a romantic affair, a family affair, or a place for friends to gather for relaxation, socializing, and play. Old Town Hot Springs is all these things, with a myriad of choices to satisfy the soaking and swimming needs of just about everyone—you would be hard-pressed to spend a day here and not come away smiling. Located in the historic town of Steamboat Springs, the facility not only serves the local community but makes for a fine weekend getaway that's sure to please each and every member of your family or group.

The Hot Springs

Heart Spring is the source of 102° water that pours at 250 gallons per minute, entering the facility at heart-shaped Heart Spring Pool, which is 3 feet, 6 inches deep, and reserved for adults. Two Spa Pools average 102°, and the Shallow Pool is about 2 feet deep and 94°. The Hot Pool is 90° to 95° in summer and 95° to 98° in winter, and features a fountain and a climbing wall.

The Slide Pool is where you'll end up after dropping from the 230-foot water-slides that wind over the soaking pools. It varies from mid-90s temps in summer to about 102° in winter. For little ones, there's a Kiddie Pool, with a zero-depth entry. Finally, the Olympic-sized Swimming, Activity & Lap Pool has eight 25-yard lap lanes that are about 80° in summer and 85° in winter; a large, inflated obstacle course; and pool toys for kids.

Top: The whimsical setting at Old Town Hot Springs is a treat for kids and their parents.
Bottom: Two 230-foot slides wind over the pools at Old Town Hot Springs.
PHOTOS BY STEWART M. GREEN

Due to the sheer size of the facility and high traffic, chlorine is added to the hot mineral spring water to keep algae—typically found in all hot spring pools—at bay. Lounging decks surround the pools, and chairs are available on a first-come, first-served basis, but you're welcome to bring your own if you like.

The Site

Old Town Hot Springs is just off the highway but set against a grassy hillside, and there are lots of trees, greenery, and potted flowers that give the impression of being far from town, amid the rolling countryside, even though you're actually within walking distance of downtown Steamboat Springs. Alongside the many pools, there's a playground and picnic area, and they even offer child care by the hour, which might come in handy if you choose to take advantage of the massage services. Inside and upstairs is the fitness center, with a weight room and cardio machine area, and you can sign up for a yoga, Spin, or Pilates class. Downstairs, there's a snack bar with seating and a service window that opens to the outside patio area. It's open in the summer and winter months only, but you're welcome to bring a cooler with your own food, snacks, and non-glass-container beverages to enjoy in the picnic area during the off-season. If you're planning a birthday, reunion, or a friendly get-together, Old Town Hot Springs has indoor space available for small parties, or you can rent the outdoor upper deck that sits high above the pool area. There's a barbecue grill, water spigot, and electricity, plus a tent and even a PA system. Call ahead for any of these private spaces, including cabanas, as they can be in high demand, especially during the summer months.

Hot Springs History

Steamboat Springs was named by French trappers who believed a hollow, resonant "chugging" sound was caused by a steamboat on the Yampa River, but the sound was actually produced by an underground chamber of compressed steam and water releasing pressure. In 1908, the chamber was "unchugged" by blasting for a railroad.

Heart Spring, the source of hot mineral water at Old Town Hot Springs, was discovered in 1874 by European settler James Crawford. In 1884, Crawford helped build a log bathhouse over the springs, and later structures included a stone building and finally a bathhouse of concrete and river stone. Heart Spring was named in 1931 by onetime property owner H. W. Gossard, who also introduced the winter carnival to the town.

Area Highlights

Steamboat Springs' motto is "Come for the winter and stay for the summer," and you'll find plenty of activities here any time of the year. In the summertime Howelsen Hill opens "The Howler," a 2,400-foot alpine slide accessed via ski lift and navigated along its twists and curves down the hill on a sled. You can kayak, canoe, tube, or raft the Yampa River; sail or angle in Stagecoach Reservoir, Lake Catamount, or Steamboat Lake; camp and hike in the Mount Zirkel and Flat Tops Wilderness Areas; and climb at Rabbit Ears Pass, Fish Creek Falls, Seedhouse Road, and throughout the Medicine Bow and Routt National Forests. There's mountain biking, horseback riding, and even roller-skating, a rodeo, a convoluted maze, miniature golf, and more summer festivals and events than you can shake a ski at.

Top: The Olympic-sized swimming pool at Old Town Hot Springs has lap lanes and more. Bottom: Old Town Hot Springs boasts a variety of pool sizes, shapes, and temperatures to suit every soaker's needs. PHOTOS BY STEWART M. GREEN

The Heart Spring Pool is a quiet place for soaking at Old Town Hot Springs. STEWART M. GREEN

There are some great walking tours here, too, including a 2-mile trek of the many natural hot springs sprinkled through town, and it starts at Old Town Hot Springs. After a big day in Steamboat Springs, you can always relax at the Botanical Gardens or enjoy Strings in the Mountains, a summer music festival and winter concert series. Or just head back to Old Town Hot Springs and sink into a pool of hot mineral water. It may be the most relaxing part of your trip.

30. STEAMBOAT SPRINGS MINERAL HOT SPRINGS WALKING TOUR

Type: Outdoor public hot springs—not for soaking.

Location: Steamboat Springs, about 160 miles northwest of Denver and 40 miles east of Craig. The walking tour is about 2 miles out and back, but you can drive between most of the springs if you like.

When to visit: 7 days a week year-round.

Access: Year-round vehicle access on public roads. ADA access to most hot springs via sidewalks and walkways.

Accommodations: None on-site, but motels and tent and RV camping are located in Glenwood Springs.

Rules: No soaking. These are small, public pools.

Services: Full services in Steamboat Springs.

Maps & GPS: *DeLorme: Colorado Atlas & Gazetteer:* p. 26, A3; *National Geographic Trails Illustrated #118, Steamboat Springs, Rabbit Ears Pass; Steamboat Springs Quadrangle.* Iron Spring 40.489733 / -106.839783; Soda Spring 40.489617 / -106.841000, Sulphur Spring 40.489617 / -106.841700, Sweetwater and Lake Springs 40.490167 / -106.842000, Steamboat Spring 40.488700 / -106.841467, Narcissus and Terrace Springs 40.488667 / -106.841333, Black Sulphur Spring 40.488750 / -106.841717, Lithia Spring 40.488450 / -106.848367, Sulphur Cave Spring 40.484200 / -106.840633, Heart Spring 40.482650 / -106.827483.

Contact: City of Steamboat Springs, (970) 879-2060, http://steamboat springs.net.

How to get there: From Denver, take I-70 West for 55 miles to exit 205 and turn right onto CO 9 North. Drive 37 miles and turn left onto US 40 West, then continue 52 miles to Steamboat Springs. Turn right on Lincoln Avenue and park in the lot on the right, across from 13th Street. Iron Spring is located here, and you can walk to the other hot springs or drive to each one separately via 13th Street, Saratoga Avenue, Lithia Springs Road, and Lincoln Avenue.

OVERVIEW

Steamboat Springs is known for its hot springs, and a leisurely walk on sidewalks and trails takes you to a dozen of them.

The Hot Springs

Iron Spring, Soda Spring, Sulphur Spring, Sweetwater and Lake Springs, Steamboat Spring, Narcissus and Terrace Springs, Black Sulphur Spring, Lithia Spring, Sulphur Cave Spring, and Heart Spring vary in appearance, odor, and minerals. You can view most of them for free, but Sulphur Cave Spring is hidden in a cave and inaccessible, and Heart Spring is located within Old Town Hot Springs, a commercial site.

Top: Black Sulphur Spring is one of twelve hot springs featured on the Steamboat Springs Mineral Hot Springs Walking Tour. Bottom: The aptly named Lithia Spring is loaded with lithium, on the Steamboat Springs Mineral Hot Springs Walking Tour. PHOTOS BY STEWART M. GREEN

Top: Steamboat Spring is a roadside spring on the Steamboat Springs Mineral Hot Springs Walking Tour. Bottom: Soda Spring, one of your many stops on the Steamboat Springs Mineral Hot Springs Walking Tour, has its own gazebo. PHOTOS BY STEWART M. GREEN

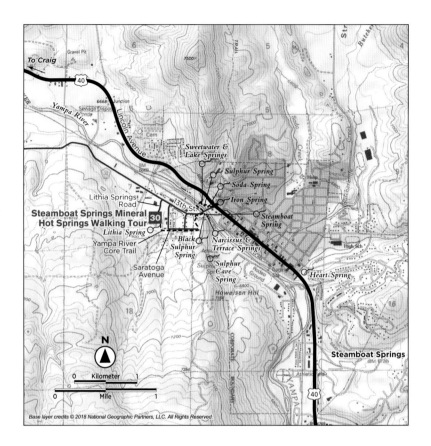

The Site

The Tread of Pioneers Museum on Oak Street has maps and guided tours of these mineral hot springs. If you'd like to tour the springs on your own, start your outing at Iron Spring, where you can park your car in the public lot. From there, cross Lincoln Avenue and head down 13th Street. On the right side of the road, you'll find Soda Spring under a gazebo, and Sulphur Spring at the northwest end of the small parking lot. Head north on the paved Yampa River Core Trail, stop by Sweetwater and Lake Springs, which feed the lake at West Lincoln Park, then backtrack a bit and cross the footbridge over the Yampa River. Turn left, continue on the paved trail, and cross 13th Street. Steamboat Spring, Narcissus and Terrace Springs, and Black Sulphur Spring are located here. Return to 13th Street and go left, then turn left onto a dirt trail that goes south to Fairview Drive. Turn right; Fairview Drive becomes Saratoga Avenue. Continue to where the road dead-ends, then take the dirt trail uphill to Lithia Spring. You can return the way you came, or continue north onto Lithia Springs Road, then turn right onto 13th Street and head back to your car.

Start your tour of Steamboat Springs Mineral Hot Springs Walking Tour at Iron Spring on Lincoln Avenue. STEWART M. GREEN

Area Highlights

Steamboat Springs has registered the trademark "Ski Town, U.S.A.," and it's a fitting title indeed: With world-class skiing at the Steamboat Ski Area, more Olympians call the town home than any other place in America! Howelsen Hill has been in continuous operation since 1915 and is home to the Steamboat Springs Winter Sports Club, an organization that's often referred to as an "Olympian factory." National competitions are common here, and the annual Steamboat Springs Winter Carnival is a five-day, citywide celebration complete with fireworks, competitions, parties, and a parade.

SOUTHWEST COLORADO HOT SPRINGS

CREEDE, PAGOSA SPRINGS, DURANGO, DOLORES, RIDGWAY, AND OURAY

Colorado's southwest boasts more hot springs than any other region in the state and is home to the deepest hot spring in the world. Commercial hot springs for every taste and budget, three wild springs, and a hot-spring walk through Pagosa Springs make the southwest a hot-springs lover's paradise. They're all located within a 4- to 7-hour drive from Colorado Springs and a 5- to 7-hour drive from Denver.

A lily-pad pond lies at the center of The Springs Resort & Spa. STEWART M. GREEN

31. 4UR RANCH & WAGON WHEEL GAP HOT SPRINGS

Type: Family-oriented outdoor and indoor public swimming and soaking, plus massage and lodging.

Location: Creede, about 15 miles northwest of South Fork.

When to visit: 7 days a week June through September. Reservations and a minimum weeklong stay are required.

Access: Vehicle access on public roads. Call ahead for ADA access details.

Accommodations: 22 rooms in Adirondack-style sleeping lodges accommodate up to 50 guests per week.

Rules: No day-soakers. Pools are for registered ranch guests only. Clothing is required.

Services: Full services in Creede and South Fork.

Map & GPS: *DeLorme: Colorado Atlas & Gazetteer:* p. 78, C3; 37.749675 / -106.831634.

Contact: 4UR Ranch, 1 Goose Creek Rd., Box 340, Creede, CO 81130; (719) 658-2202; www.4urranch.com. Call or visit website for rates, reservations, and hours of operation.

How to get there: From South Fork, take CO 149 North for 13 miles and turn left onto Goose Creek Road. Continue 1.6 miles to 4UR Ranch & Wagon Wheel Gap Hot Springs, on the left.

OVERVIEW

The Silver Thread Scenic Byway between South Fork and Creede winds along the Rio Grande River through a narrow canyon known as Wagon Wheel Gap. North of the canyon, Goose Creek drops from the Continental Divide and meanders through a slender valley before emptying into the Rio Grande. Here a seasonal, ranch-resort-style vacation getaway offers swimming, soaking, and outdoor recreation featuring 6 miles of tailwater and many miles of trails.

The Hot Springs

The spa area at 4UR Ranch houses a large outdoor pool surrounded by wooden decking and privacy for quiet sunning and swimming. The pool water is not hot spring water, but it is geothermally heated, so you can enjoy an early morning or evening swim.

Inside the spa, soak in a sunken tub of 106° mineral water fed by an on-site natural hot spring, where water emerges at 136°.

The Site

Generations of guests return to 4UR Ranch every year, and so reservations should be made far in advance. The accommodations are not rustic, but luxury-style living with gourmet cuisine and a high level of service. While your stay is all-inclusive, massage services at the spa and alcoholic beverages at the bar are a little extra.

In line with the ranch resort theme, 4UR Ranch offers outdoor recreation and activities for adults and for the kids. There are children's programs, hiking, and

Top: Enjoy an early morning or late night swim in the geothermally warmed waters at the 4UR Ranch pool. Bottom: Hot spring water at 4UR Ranch comes from two springs, and you can view them with a hike around the ranch. PHOTOS BY STEWART M. GREEN

The indoor hot springs soaking tub at 4UR Ranch is fed by an on-site natural hot spring.
EMILY MINTON REDFIELD - COURTESY 4UR RANCH

painting workshops, plus all the outdoor activities you would expect at a Colorado ranch in the San Juan Mountains.

Hot Springs History

The 4UR Ranch originated in the 1880s as the Hot Springs Hotel at Wagon Wheel Gap. The hot springs were called "Little Medicine" by the Ute Indians, and by the turn of the century, General William Palmer had redeveloped the property as a health resort to rival the spas of Europe. After his death in 1909, the resort was bought and sold a few times until 1972, when the Leavell family purchased the property and returned it to its luxury status. Three generations later, they are still welcoming guests to the Little Medicine hot springs.

Area Highlights

You may never want to leave 4UR Ranch, but if you feel like getting away for a few hours, drive the Silver Thread Scenic and Historic Byway north to Creede. Just north of the town, take your high-clearance 4WD vehicle on the Bachelor Loop Historic Tour, a rugged 17-mile drive through ghost towns with scenic views all around. If you have more time, head west for about an hour to North Clear Creek Falls, the most photographed waterfall in Colorado. Then catch a show at the Creede Repertory Theatre. Dinner and a hot soak will be waiting for you back at 4UR Ranch.

32. PIEDRA RIVER HOT SPRINGS

Type: Wild outdoor public soaking, plus primitive camping.

Location: Piedra Area, San Juan National Forest, with the trailhead about 30 miles west of Pagosa Springs, and the hike to the hot springs 3 miles round-trip.

When to visit: Summer and fall, as the road to the trailhead is closed to motorized vehicles other than snowmobiles during winter and spring.

Access: Summer and fall access to trailhead on public roads; during winter and spring the road is closed about 0.5 mile north of the highway, requiring an additional 6-mile trek each way via snowshoes, skis, or snowmobile. Snowmobiles are not allowed 1 mile past the trailhead, in the Piedra Area. No ADA access.

Accommodations: Primitive tent camping only in the Piedra Area; additional camping is located at the trailhead, and motels are located in Pagosa Springs.

Rules: Clothing is optional. San Juan National Forest and Piedra Area regulations apply.

Services: Full services in Pagosa Springs.

Maps & GPS: *DeLorme: Colorado Atlas & Gazetteer*: p. 87, B7; *National Geographic Trails Illustrated #145*, Pagosa Springs, Bayfield; Devil Mountain Quadrangle. Trailhead 37.303000 / -107.336450; hot springs, 37.312950 / -107.344150.

Contact: USDA Forest Service, San Juan National Forest, Pagosa Ranger District, 180 Pagosa St., PO Box 310, Pagosa Springs, CO 81147; (970) 264-2268; www.fs.usda.gov/sanjuan.

How to get there: From Pagosa Springs, take US 160 West for 22 miles and turn right onto FR 622/Archuleta CR 166/First Fork Road. Travel about 6.5 miles to the junction with Monument Park Road. Sheep Creek Trailhead parking is on your left.

OVERVIEW

Piedra River Hot Springs is a rare, easily accessed wild spring, so tread lightly on your visit. You'll pass through a ponderosa pine forest, where you can sniff the bark and try to decide whether it smells like caramel or vanilla. There are fields of yellow goldenrod, blue and lavender lupine, daisies, wild rose, and thistle. Tiny pink and white blossoms dot the landscape among wild grasses and great blocks of sandstone and limestone. There's poison ivy, too, so keep to the trail and enjoy the hues and the views; you'll soon be soaking in natural pools along the riverbed.

The Hot Springs

Located on the west side of the Piedra River in the San Juan National Forest, these pools are fed by a spring that sprouts from the riverbank at about 108°, plus hidden underwater springs that bubble up from the pool bottoms. Soakers dig as many as a dozen pools along the river, separating them with stacked rocks to keep the hot spring water in and the cold river water out.

The Site

Piedra River Hot Springs is accessed via Sheep Creek Trail. There is parking at the trailhead, and the trail starts off gently enough before dropping sharply about 600 feet. There are many switchbacks in the steepest sections, though, making this a quick and easy downhill hike and an only slightly less pleasant uphill one. It's roughly 0.8 mile down to the riverbank, where there's a large fire ring and rough-hewn wooden seating to your left, but the trail to the springs goes north, to the right. Follow it for another 0.8 mile to a large, flat campsite and then straight down to the pools. The trail is clear and easy to follow the entire way. Your total hike will be 3 miles round-trip, so bring water and snacks, proper clothing and footwear, and sunscreen. Like most undeveloped hot spring pools, the usual attire at Piedra Hot Springs is no attire at all, so don't be surprised if you come upon soakers and sunbathers au naturel along the riverbank and in the pools. Likewise, if you choose to enjoy the springs in your most natural state, keep in mind that families may be visiting the area; let your common sense guide you in using proper discretion on those occasions.

SAN JUAN NATIONAL FOREST AND PIEDRA AREA

The Piedra Area, which begins 1 mile into the hike to Piedra River Hot Springs, was designated as such in 1993. Sixty-thousand acres within the Piedra Road-less Area make up the Piedra Area, which shares many of the same protections enjoyed by Colorado wilderness areas. If you visit Piedra River Hot Springs, follow the regulations that apply to ensure the hot springs and surrounding lands remain pristine and accessible. Bicycles and motorized vehicles, including snowmobiles, are not allowed. Don't cut the switchbacks, as that destroys vegetation, causes erosion, and damages the existing trail. Camp at least 100 feet from water sources, and dispose of all wash water at least 200 feet from the river and hot springs. Bury human waste far from the river and carry out everything else, including toilet paper and any other personal products. Plan ahead by packing in enough plastic and resealable bags to accommodate your trash, and if you're camping, pack in a trowel for human-waste burial. When traveling with a pet, be sure to adhere to these same principles so as not to sully the trails and waters. Observe fire restrictions and never, ever leave a fire unattended. Do not use live trees or green or rotting wood, as these resources are critical to the sustained vitality of the area. Use only dead wood and existing fire rings to avoid additional impact to the land, extinguish campfires completely before your departure, and ensure the ashes are cold.

There are many weeds in the Piedra Area with seeds that can stick like Velcro, so keep to the trail and remove any sticks and seeds from your clothing before you leave the area, so you don't spread the weeds to other locations. Finally, natural, undeveloped hot springs are a rare treat in Colorado, so keep your visits to Piedra Hot Springs short, few, and far between to avoid overuse of the area. These hot springs have been around for generations, but we must treat them gently and ethically if we are to continue to share them with generations of hot springs enthusiasts for years to come.

Top: Piedra River Hot Springs are located on the west side of the Piedra River in the San Juan National Forest. Bottom: Soakers separate the pools at Piedra River Hot Springs with stacked rocks to keep the hot spring water in and the cold river water out. SUSAN JOY PAUL

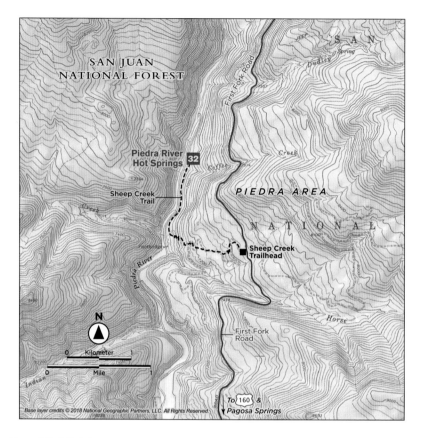

Base layer credits © 2018 National Geographic Partners, LLC. All Rights Reserved.

Area Highlights

There's plenty to do in Archuleta County, but once you've discovered the Piedra Area and adjacent Piedra Roadless Area, you may want to spend another day, or longer, exploring this part of Southwest Colorado. With more than 100,000 acres of combined roadless and special management areas, and miles of rivers and tributaries, there's plenty of hiking, camping, and backpacking to enjoy. The rangers at the Pagosa Ranger District Office will answer your questions about access, camping, and restrictions, and there are maps and guidebooks for purchase as well.

West of Pagosa Springs, the Chimney Rock Archaeological Area makes for a pleasant side trip. Lying on more than 4,000 acres in the San Juan National Forest, Chimney Rock was home to the ancestors of modern Pueblo Indians, and more than 200 ancient homes, work farms, and ceremonial buildings have been discovered on the grounds. In 1970, the area was designated an Archaeological Area and National Historic Site. It's open from May 15 to September 30, access is free, and for a fee you can get a guided tour or an audio kiva tour.

33. RAINBOW HOT SPRINGS

Type: Wild outdoor public soaking, plus primitive camping.

Location: Weminuche Wilderness Area, San Juan National Forest, with the trailhead about 18 miles northeast of Pagosa Springs and the hike to the hot spring about 10 miles round-trip.

When to visit: Summer and fall, as the road to the trailhead is closed to motorized vehicles during winter and early spring.

Access: Summer and fall access to trailhead on public roads; during winter and early spring, the road is closed from highway to trailhead, requiring an additional 7.5-mile trek each way via snowshoes, skis, or snowmobile. Snowmobiles are not allowed past the trailhead. No ADA access.

Accommodations: Primitive tent camping only in the Weminuche Wilderness Area. Additional tent camping and RV campsites are located along the road to the trailhead, and motels are located 18 miles southwest in Pagosa Springs.

Rules: Clothing is optional. San Juan National Forest and Weminuche Wilderness Area regulations apply.

Services: Full services in Pagosa Springs.

Maps & GPS: *DeLorme: Colorado Atlas & Gazetteer*: p. 78, E2; *National Geographic Trails Illustrated #140*, Weminuche Wilderness; South River Peak and Saddle Mountain Quadrangles. Trailhead 37.457717 / -106.919450; hot springs, 37.508933 / -106.947900.

Contact: USDA Forest Service, San Juan National Forest, Pagosa Ranger District, 180 Pagosa St., PO Box 310, Pagosa Springs, CO 81147; (970) 264-2268; www.fs.usda.gov/sanjuan.

How to get there: From Pagosa Springs, take US 160 northeast for 15 miles, then turn left onto West Fork Road at mile marker 158. Travel about 3 miles on West Fork Road, bearing left toward the West Fork Campground, and then to the right toward the West Fork Trailhead. The trailhead is located between the restroom and information kiosk.

OVERVIEW

The hike to Rainbow Hot Springs is the second longest in this book, but it's a beautiful trek on a nice trail with lots of ups and downs. You'll travel through dense spruce and aspen groves, over the rushing waters of West Fork rivulets on sturdy bridges, and across downed tree trunks and branches. There are muddy sections, too, with a smattering of rocks to keep you high and dry. If you are not in good shape or used to hiking Colorado trails, this may be too daunting a trip, but for those accustomed to long hikes around the state, this is a moderate trek to a fine destination.

The Hot Springs

Like all natural, undeveloped pools, the conditions at Rainbow Hot Springs vary greatly depending on the season, weather, and how much effort has gone into maintaining them. You will usually find at least one pool for soaking beneath a hot spring that pours down the riverbank, and more pools may exist, fed by runoff from the

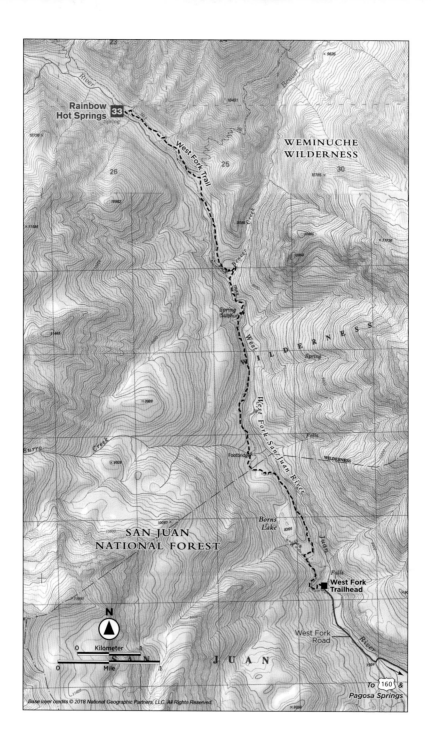

Rainbow
Hot Springs 33
Spring

West Fork Trail

26

25

WEMINUCHE
WILDERNESS

30

Spring
(Sulphur)

W I L D E R N E S S

West Fork San Juan River

Spring

Falls

WILDERNESS

Footbridge

SAN JUAN
NATIONAL FOREST

Borns
Lake

West Fork
Trailhead

Falls

N

Kilometer

Mile

S A N

J U A N

West Fork
Road

River

To 160 &
Pagosa Springs

Base layer credits © 2018 National Geographic Partners, LLC. All Rights Reserved.

Like all natural, undeveloped pools, the conditions at Rainbow Hot Springs vary greatly depending on the season, weather, and how much effort has gone into maintaining them.
SUSAN JOY PAUL

main pool and underground seepage. Farther up the trail, a couple of warm pools are located in a flat grassy area left of the trail.

The Site

The hike to Rainbow Hot Springs begins at the West Fork Trailhead, and the first mile is on a dirt road and trail that crosses through private property. This section of the trail is well signed as "Rainbow Trail," but the distances noted on the signs are slightly off—expect a longer hike. Although the trail appears on a map to be about 4.5 miles each way, the ups and downs in elevation add almost 0.5 mile in both directions, for a nearly 10-mile-long round-trip hike. Plan accordingly. The private property here is off-limits and also well marked very accurately, so keep to the signed route. As wide road turns to narrow trail, the route hovers high above the San Juan River, and there is occasional but dramatic exposure along the soft shoulder to the right side of the trail. If you are traveling with children or pets, keep them close at hand as a fall here would be extremely dangerous and perhaps deadly. Soon enough you'll be back on safe footing, though, and crossing a field of skunk cabbage. The first mile of this hike is also where you'll experience the greatest continuous rise in elevation from the trailhead, so don't be discouraged as the trail soon enters the Weminuche Wilderness Area, levels out, and finally relents in a gentle up-and-down trek through spruce-filled forest.

SAN JUAN NATIONAL FOREST AND WEMINUCHE WILDERNESS AREA

Located in the Weminuche Wilderness Area, Rainbow Hot Springs enjoys certain protections afforded the land and waters of this area. The Weminuche Wilderness was designated as such in 1975 and expanded to its current size of nearly half a million acres by Colorado Wilderness Acts in 1980 and 1993. Travelers should respect the USDA Forest Service's regulations to protect the land and ensure continued access. Bicycles and motorized vehicles are not allowed the entire length of the West Fork Trail. If you choose to have a campfire, observe fire restrictions and never, ever leave a fire unattended. Do not use live trees or green or rotting wood, as these resources are critical to the sustained vitality of the area. Use only dead wood and existing fire rings to avoid additional impact to the land, extinguish campfires completely before your departure, and ensure the ashes are cold.

Camp at least 100 feet from water sources, and dispose of all wash water at least 200 feet from the river and hot springs. Bury human waste far from the river and carry out everything else, including toilet paper and any other personal products. Plan ahead by packing in enough plastic and resealable bags to accommodate your trash, and if you're camping, pack in a trowel for human-waste burial. When traveling with a pet, be sure to adhere to these same principles so as not to sully the trails and waters. Your pet should be on leash or voice command, and there is no animal grazing allowed. Finally, undeveloped, free hot spring pools are rare and account for a very small percentage of the hot springs in Colorado, so keep your visits to Rainbow Hot Springs short, few, and far between, to avoid overuse of the area and ensure continued enjoyment by future generations.

From the trailhead, you'll enter the wilderness area about 1.5 miles into your hike. Just past the wilderness boundary, you'll reach the first bridge, the Burro Creek Bridge, and enjoy your first crossing of the West Fork of the San Juan River. If you're ready for a break, there's a big tree trunk coming up soon, along the side of the road in the shade, and it makes a nice seat for a rest and a snack. Continue up the trail and cross a rivulet on thick branches. The trail climbs again, more steeply now, ascending to the highest point of the route, where you may want to stop for a moment to catch your breath and enjoy the views. A steep and loose downhill section follows, but thankfully it's short. Continue on and cross the West Fork Bridge and, shortly after, the Beaver Creek Bridge. Soon you'll come upon the junction with the Beaver Creek Trail; that trail switchbacks sharply up to the right, but it's not maintained, not safe, and it won't take you to the hot springs. Instead, you'll want to continue straight ahead on the West Fork (Rainbow) Trail.

Along the final mile to the hot springs, there's an easy and scenic water crossing. Pause here and look upstream to your right: There's a wondrous waterfall cascading down from a cliff and spilling into the river! You'll find the last river crossing soon after this one, and it may be the trickiest, with a jumble of rocks and branches to assist you across. The trail then rises slightly, curves to the right, and enters a flat area with old campsites. Look to the left of the trail for a big spruce tree with an orange blaze

Hike a little past the hot springs at Rainbow Hot Springs to a couple of warm pools in a grassy area. SUSAN JOY PAUL

painted on it. Take the trail to the left of the tree. Be warned: This is the steepest, loosest section of the route, dropping rapidly down to the river. The terrain is slippery ball-bearing-like scree on hardpan, and there is little traction. Cut to the right, toward the visible pools below. If you continue past the hot spring a short distance on the trail, you'll find a small meadow and a couple of warm pots off the trail, along the riverbed.

For the hike to Rainbow Hot Springs, be sure to bring plenty of water and snacks, proper clothing and footwear, sunscreen, and a rain jacket. You may also consider

Warm pools dot the riverbank at Rainbow Hot Springs. SUSAN JOY PAUL

trekking poles to take some of the stress off your knees and assist with balance on the river crossings. Typical attire at Rainbow Hot Springs is no attire at all, so expect to see soakers and sunbathers alike in their natural states, along the riverbank and in the pools. Likewise, if you choose to soak au naturel, keep in mind that families may be visiting the area; let your common sense guide you in using proper discretion on those occasions.

Area Highlights

A visit to Rainbow Hot Springs is just one way to enjoy views of the San Juan River. For a more up-close-and-personal experience, consider enlisting a local guide service for kayaking, whitewater rafting, or tubing. Outfitters will accommodate you on a walk-in basis, but reservations are usually a good idea, especially for large groups. For most activities, little or no prior experience is required, and they can provide you with all the gear—helmets, life jackets, and so on—but plan on bringing your own water shoes, sunscreen, sunglasses and retainer, hat, comfortable clothing, and a plastic or metal water bottle. If you do forget something, you can probably buy it at the guide shop or somewhere else in Pagosa Springs.

Pagosa Springs and Archuleta County offer plenty of activities to keep you busy in the days before and after your hike to Rainbow Hot Springs, but with 492,418 acres of backcountry and 475 miles of trails, you may want to stick around the Weminuche Wilderness Area for more hiking, camping, backpacking, and mountaineering. A visit to the Pagosa Ranger District Office in Pagosa Springs will help to answer all your questions about access, camping, and restrictions, and there are plenty of maps and guidebooks for purchase there as well.

34. THE SPRINGS RESORT & SPA

Type: Family-oriented, resort-style hot spring with public soaking, swimming, spa, luxury hotel, motel, conference center, concierge service and swimwear shop.

Location: Pagosa Springs, about 60 miles southwest of Del Norte.

When to visit: 7 days a week year-round.

Access: Year-round vehicle access on public roads. Call ahead for ADA access details.

Accommodations: 79 rooms total, from standard motel accommodations with some pet-friendly rooms to luxury suites in a 29-room boutique hotel.

Rules: Day-soakers welcome. Clothing is required. No smoking, no alcohol, no glass containers. No pets at the pools.

Services: Full services in Pagosa Springs.

Map & GPS: *DeLorme: Colorado Atlas & Gazetteer:* p. 88, C2; 37.265884 / -107.010446.

Contact: The Springs Resort & Spa; 165 Hot Springs Blvd., Pagosa Springs, CO 81147; (970) 264-4168; www .pagosahotsprings.com. Call or visit website for rates, reservations, and hours of operation.

How to get there: From Main Street/ Pagosa Street in Pagosa Springs, go west and turn left onto Hermosa Street, and continue onto Hot Springs Boulevard. The Springs Resort & Spa is on the right side of the road.

OVERVIEW

The Springs Resort & Spa is a hot springs wonderland of outdoor soaking and swimming pools situated along the east bank of the San Juan River. Twenty-three individual hot pools cling to the riverbank, sidle up to natural mineral formations, and rise in clusters atop stone and concrete landings. The Mediterranean-style bathhouse and stunning pink-and-orange natural travertine fountainhead provide a pastel backdrop for the vivid blue, green, and aqua mineral waters, and a big goldfish-and-lily-pad pond lies at the center, traversed by a submerged hanging boardwalk. A luxury hotel, conference space, swimming pool, Jacuzzi pool, and full-service spa and salon add up to a dazzling resort with lots of choices for hot springs soakers, swimmers, and overnight guests.

The Hot Springs

Once you get past the sumptuous eye candy of the roaring river, crystal pools, and artfully terraced mix of natural and man-made baths, it's time to find your hot pool and, with twenty-three pools, you have plenty of options. Visit Lobster Pot for a steamy soak. If you prefer your hot springs mingled with cold river water, step into Crick Pool, Michael Degree, or The Burg. Tucked high into the southwest corner of the resort are Cozy Cove, Top o' the Mornin', Summer Breeze, Twilight, and Riverbend, along with the adults-only, riverside Serendipity pool. The second adults-only pool, Clouds in My Coffee, sits high above Golden Pond, while The Cliffs nestles beside it. Venetian, Marco Polo, Waterfall, Aspen, and Paradise hug the San Juan River, and Overlook, Sunset Social Club, Tranquility, Boulder, Treasure, and Columbine lie north of the pond, near the bathhouse. This is a quiet, relaxed atmosphere.

The family-oriented, recreational area on the northeast side of the site includes a nonmineral Jacuzzi pool, Dancing Waters, which flows into a large swimming pool, The Blue Lagoon, the only pool where toys are allowed. A big-screen theater at the water's edge airs movies three nights a week.

All but the two pools in the rec area are fed by on-site natural hot springs, no chemicals are added, and the water flows in and back out continuously, for complete replacement about every 2 hours. Each pool is signed with its name and temperature posted.

The Site

In spite of all the trimmings, the real highlight of these hot springs is the natural scenery—it's not possible to upstage the bordering San Juan River to the west, San Juan Mountains to the north, or the centerpiece of The Springs Resort & Spa, an enormous mound of cascading, petrified travertine. However, the hot pools and paved walkways, low walls and fire pits of handlaid stonework, and pretty smattering of green trees and rock gardens blend well and do the setting justice. There's a gazebo in the pool area that sells cold beverages, including beer and wine, and snacks, and you can bring in your own food, too, but glass containers and outside alcoholic beverages are not allowed. There are umbrella-topped tables and chairs that offer a respite from this sunbathed area of the state. The lower San Juan Basin averages about 300 days of sunshine each year, so before you stretch out on that lounge chair for a sundrenched nap, be sure to grab a floppy hat, sunscreen, and sunglasses.

The spa at the Springs Resort has an extensive menu, offering everything from the standard massage, facial, and body treatments to reflexology and chiropractic services, spray-tanning, eyelash extensions, and champagne pedicures. There are plenty of overnight accommodations available, too, and the resort uses geothermal energy extensively throughout the premises.

The original hotel—the Springs Resort Hotel—has fifty rooms of various configurations, including some pet-friendly rooms. The Luxury Suites Hotel has twenty-nine rooms and was the first Gold LEED–certified hotel in the state. A Gold LEED (Leadership in Energy and Environmental Design) designation is an internationally recognized standard and denotes adherence to exceptional requirements for energy efficiency and environmental sustainability. Geothermal and groundwater systems heat and cool all of the buildings at the resort and provide the hot water as well. Even the handrails and walkways around the bathhouse are heated this way, to help melt wintertime snow and ice and prevent spills. While both hotels are well appointed, the newer Luxury Suites Hotel has an understated and very classy Tara-like opulence that's apparent when you first step through the doors. Dark woods gleam and golden lighting glistens, while woven rugs lead the way up a central grand staircase. Underneath the old-world style is modern convenience too: The rooms feature marble countertops, stainless-steel appliances, and Jacuzzi tubs. Plump brocade pillows adorn

Top: The Mediterranean-style bathhouse and stunning pink-and-orange natural travertine fountainhead provide a pastel backdrop for the vivid blue, green, and aqua mineral waters at The Springs Resort & Spa. Bottom: The Springs Resort & Spa is a hot springs wonderland of outdoor soaking and swimming pools situated along the east bank of the San Juan River. PHOTOS BY STEWART M. GREEN

the beds, and private balconies offer views of the mountains, river, and pool area. The Springs Resort & Spa has seen many celebrity guests over the years: John Wayne is said to have frequented the springs while filming *The Cowboys*, and Oprah Winfrey taped a segment for her show here in 2006. In fact, you can book a night in the "O Room" if you like, and complete the media-mogul experience with luxurious spa and salon treatments. The concierge service will arrange tours for you, including biking, hiking, visiting ancient ruins, river rafting, or sitting in a balloon basket and floating high above Pagosa Springs. We may not all be Oscar winners or even nominees like Wayne or Winfrey, but sometimes it's fun to feel like one.

Hot Springs History

In the mid-1800s, the area became a destination for people seeking health benefits from these waters, and in 1877 Pagosa was designated a township by the US government. After several booms and busts, the hot springs resort was purchased by the present owners, Nerissa and Keely Whittington. Over a couple of decades, they developed the once-dilapidated roadside motel and its hot tubs that were filled by a garden hose, into a world-class resort and spa. The Springs and surrounding public and protected lands at Pagosa Springs draw many tourists and seasonal guests to the area.

Area Highlights

Surrounded by the San Juan National Forest, Pagosa Springs offers year-round outdoor recreational fun. Take advantage of concierge service at the Springs Resort & Spa or hire a local outfitter for adventures in hiking, camping, mountain biking, rock climbing, rafting, tubing, horseback riding, dogsledding, skijoring, and snowmobiling.

In the summer, the town celebrates July 4th over several days with a carnival, arts and crafts festival, a walk/run called the "Star Spangled Shuffle," and a parade. The Springs Resort & Spa is the perfect place to view the night's fireworks. In mid-September, the three-day Pagosa Food & Wine Fest includes a balloon festival and you can watch the hot air balloons rise above the hot springs from the resort. In the wintertime, you're a hop, skip, and slalom from Wolf Creek Ski Resort, home to 1,600 acres of skiable high country. Wolf Creek averages 465 inches of natural snowfall annually and the ski season lasts about five months. Enjoy downhill skiing and snowboarding and cross-country tours. After a day on the slopes, go from chilly powder to steamy pool with an après ski soak at the Springs Resort & Spa.

Facing page, top left: A travertine fountain borders the pool area at The Springs Resort & Spa. Top right: Twenty-three individual hot pools cling to the riverbank, sidle up to natural mineral formations, and rise in clusters atop stone and concrete landings at The Springs Resort & Spa. Bottom: Soak your worries away at The Springs Resort & Spa. PHOTOS BY STEWART M. GREEN

35. **HEALING WATERS RESORT & SPA**

Type: Family-oriented outdoor and indoor public swimming and soaking, plus massage and spa services and lodging.

Location: Pagosa Springs, about 60 miles southwest of Del Norte.

When to visit: 7 days a week year-round.

Access: Year-round vehicle access on public roads. Call ahead for ADA access details.

Accommodations: 14-room motel, 3 cabins, a bunkhouse that sleeps 6, 4 RV spaces.

Rules: Day-soakers welcome. Clothing required in community pool and tub, optional in gender-segregated bathhouse hot baths. No smoking, no alcohol, and no pets at the pool or around any soaking areas; no smoking and no pets in the motel or cabins; pets in the RV area must be leashed.

Services: Full services in Pagosa Springs.

Map & GPS: *DeLorme: Colorado Atlas & Gazetteer*: p. 88, C2; 37.266164 / -107.009223.

Contact: Healing Waters Resort & Spa, 317 Hot Springs Blvd., Pagosa Springs, CO 81147; (970) 264-5910; www.pshotsprings.com. Call or visit website for rates, reservations, and hours of operation.

How to get there: From Main Street/Pagosa Street in Pagosa Springs, go west and turn left onto Hermosa Street, and continue onto Hot Springs Boulevard. Healing Waters is on the left side of the road.

OVERVIEW

Healing Waters Resort & Spa enjoys a long history as a family-owned establishment that attracts loyal locals and out-of-town guests alike. Neat and clean, with a simplicity harking back to the 1950s, the status quo development lends a feeling of comfort and predictability that's sometimes lost over the ages at more progressive hot springs sites, and it may leave you feeling wistful for days gone by. The swimming pool offers a place to play, the hot tub a place to gather, and the bathhouse a place to relax, and you'll want to try all three to make the most of your visit to Healing Waters.

The Hot Springs

The big swimming pool is about 75 feet long, slopes from 3 to 6 feet deep, and is maintained at at about 90° during the summer and 95° in winter. Tucked around the corner and behind the bathhouses, the aboveground hot tub has trees for privacy and a sunning space with lounge chairs. The tub is about 4 feet deep and 103° to 106°.

The gender-specific, adults-only bathhouses have big, sunken hot baths for soaking, and the water is 108° to 112°. All three options at Healing Waters—the pool, hot tub, and hot baths—are filled with 100 percent hot spring mineral water, no chlorine or other chemicals added. They are drained and power-washed regularly.

Top: Everybody loves the big hot springs pool at Healing Waters Resort & Spa!
Bottom: Steam rises into the evening air at Healing Waters Resort & Spa.
PHOTOS BY STEWART M. GREEN

The Site

There's plenty of overnight lodging at Healing Waters, including a fourteen-room motel, three cabins, a bunkhouse for six, and four spots for RVs. None of the accommodations have summertime window-units, the double queen rooms in the motel have ceiling fans, and the cabins feature large windows all around for cross breezes and front porches where you can sit out in the morning and evening hours with a hot cup of coffee or a cool beverage and enjoy the fresh air. The motel rooms hold up to four guests each, and some have kitchenettes. The cabins hold up to six people, and the RV spots have full hookups and pull-throughs. There's cable TV and Wi-Fi available throughout the facility, and overnight guests are allowed free usage of all swimming and soaking pools. The on-site spa offers body treatments including sugar scrubs, butter wraps, acupressure, facials, and a variety of massages.

Hot Springs History

Navajos and Utes soaked at Pagosa Springs long before white settlers came to town. Ultimately, due to the continual influx of settlers, treaties between the US government and the Utes collapsed with repeated abuses of the trust, and the Indians were exiled. Nearly a century later, and after passing through many more hands, the Healing Waters Resort & Spa came under the ownership of the Giordano family and has since enjoyed a reputation not as a battleground, but rather a peaceful place for fun and relaxation.

Area Highlights

The San Juan River runs right through Pagosa Springs, and you can enjoy it by raft, kayak, or tube. Likewise, the nearby San Juan Mountains provide endless trails, wilderness camping, and mountaineering adventures. Stop by the Pagosa Springs Chamber of Commerce or Pagosa Ranger District office for information, maps, and guidebooks, or arrange a trip with a local guide company.

Enjoy a quiet evening at Healing Waters Resort & Spa. STEWART M. GREEN

In the summertime visit Chimney Rock Archaeological Area on the southwest side of town; in the winter Wolf Creek Ski Area—with an average 40 feet of snow annually—opens just 25 miles to the north. If you want to get out and stretch your legs any time of the year, consider a short, moderate, or overnight hike to a nearby waterfall. Trails to Silver Falls, Treasure Falls, Piedra Falls, Lean Creek Falls, Fourmile Falls, and A Waterfall Without a Name vary from 0.25 mile to 26 miles round-trip, and your reward is a sparkling tumble of natural beauty and a fine backdrop for your vacation photos. Bring a picnic lunch and a camera, and leave nothing behind.

36. OVERLOOK HOT SPRINGS SPA

Type: Cozy, quiet, indoor and outdoor public and private soaking, plus massage.

Location: Pagosa Springs, about 60 miles southwest of Del Norte.

When to visit: 7 days a week year-round.

Access: Year-round vehicle access on public roads. Call ahead for ADA access details.

Accommodations: None on-site, but tent and RV camping and motels are located in Pagosa Springs.

Rules: Day-soaker facility. Clothing is required in public tubs, optional in private tubs. No smoking, no drugs, no glass containers, and no pets allowed.

Services: Full services in Pagosa Springs.

Map & GPS: *DeLorme: Colorado Atlas & Gazetteer:* p. 88, C2; 37.267075 / -107.010844.

Contact: Overlook Hot Springs Spa, 432 Pagosa St., Pagosa Springs, CO 81147; (970) 264-4040; www.overlook hotsprings.com. Call or visit website for rates and hours of operation.

How to get there: In Pagosa Springs, take US 160 to Pagosa Street; Overlook Hot Springs is on the right side of the road.

OVERVIEW

Overlook Hot Springs Spa is the newest hot spring spot in Pagosa Springs and a great example of the variety of soaking options in the area. The Victorian-style building blends right in with the surrounding shops on Pagosa Street, but hidden inside, from the ground floor to the sunny rooftop, fifteen steamy soaking tubs await.

The Hot Springs

Three rooftop tubs, seven outdoor courtyard tubs, three side-by-side indoor tubs, and two private indoor tubs offer lots of choices for the discriminating soaker.

The rooftop pools are sunken and offer views of the San Juan Mountains and the town of Pagosa Springs. Between soaks, you can relax on the deck with an adult beverage—beer or wine—and watch the clouds go by. The hot mineral water in these tubs varies from about 90° in the summer to between 103° and 106° in the winter. There's also a dry sauna and an adults-only Jacuzzi tub.

Courtyard tubs and a cool plunge are perfect for parties at Overlook Hot Springs Spa. STEWART M. GREEN

Three rooftop tubs, seven outdoor courtyard tubs, three side-by-side indoor tubs, and two private indoor tubs offer lots of choices for the discriminating soaker at Overlook Hot Springs Spa. STEWART M. GREEN

The indoor soaking tubs range from about 104° to 108°, and the environment there is calm and quiet. The private, clothing-optional soaking tubs fit four or five people and are available for rent by the hour. Reservations are required for these tubs, and guests can request their personal temperature preference.

Finally, seven courtyard tubs and a cool plunge are perfect for parties. Canopies offer shade, and the area is fenced in and private.

The waters here are 122° at the source but cooled via a cooling tower.

The Site

Overlook Hot Springs Spa offers massages, scrubs, and other treatments in a relaxed atmosphere. Ask about special pricing on massage and soaking bundles. The rooftop is a more social place, and you can buy snacks, drinks, beer and wine. The entire rooftop area is available to rent for private occasions.

Area Highlights

Step out of the Overlook and smack dab into the middle of Pagosa Springs. Grab a bite at a local restaurant—there are plenty within walking distance—then keep the good vibe going with a scenic drive. Wolf Creek Pass, Windy Point, Blanco Basin, and the Plumtaw-Piedra Loop are all accessible by passenger car.

If you opt for the East Fork Road to Elwood Pass, you'll want a high-clearance 4WD vehicle, good driving skills, and great weather. East Fork Road is located off US 160, 10 miles east of Pagosa Springs. About 8 miles up the road, pull into the lot on the left side of the road and take a short hike up to Silver Falls. Then get back in your car and continue driving, bearing left at the fork, toward Elwood Pass. The road gets very narrow, rocky, and steep. You'll pass Joe Mann Creek and Black Diamond Mine, and go over the Continental Divide to Summitville, an old abandoned mining town.

37. THE SAN JUAN RIVER WALK

Type: Outdoor public hot springs.

Location: Pagosa Springs, about 60 miles southwest of Del Norte. The river walk is about 2 miles out and back, or a 1.7 mile loop, and there is parking at each end.

When to visit: 7 days a week year-round.

Access: Year-round vehicle access on public roads. ADA access to most hot springs on paved walkway.

Accommodations: None on-site, but tent and RV camping and motels are located in Pagosa Springs.

Rules: Clothing is required. Even though these are wild springs, they are in a public place. No motor vehicles on the river walk, but bicycles are allowed. Pedestrians have right of way.

Services: Full services in Pagosa Springs.

Maps & GPS: *DeLorme: Colorado Atlas & Gazetteer:* p. 88, C2; *National Geographic Trails Illustrated #145,* Pagosa Springs, Bayfield; Pagosa Springs Quadrangle. Parking 37.267280 / -107.007787, hot springs located at 37.267120 / -107.009378, 37.266919 / -107.010141, 37.266472 / -107.010663, 37.266300 / -107.010746, 37.264377 / -107.014017, 37.263821 / -107.014272.

Contact: Town of Pagosa Springs, Parks & Recreation, (970) 264-4151, www.pagosasprings.co.gov.

How to get there: From Main Street/Pagosa Street in Pagosa Springs, go west and turn left on Hermosa Street and left again to stay on Hermosa Street, then right onto Hermosa Alley West and right into the parking lot at the Pagosa Springs Town Park. The San Juan River Walk starts at the south end of the lot and heads west (right) on a paved walkway.

OVERVIEW

Not all the hot springs in Pagosa Springs are contained at commercial sites or accessed by long walks in the woods. This scenic stroll along the San Juan River in downtown Pagosa Springs is dotted with sulfurous springs for smelling, soaking, and sightseeing.

The Hot Springs

Natural hot springs along the river walk vary from soaking pools to small fountains and large, steamy ponds. Some are suitable for soaking, while others are just for viewing. Their sources range from underwater hot springs to runoff from nearby commercial sites, and the conditions vary with the season and the weather.

The Site

You can start this hike at the north end, from Town Park, or at the south end near the Pagosa Springs Municipal Court. From Town Park, cross the footbridge to Mary Fisher Park and go right on the paved walkway. The first hot spring you'll see is on the far riverbank; Hot Springs Boulevard spans the river. Just before the bridge, a pipe pours water into a large pool protected by piled-up rocks along the river.

The San Juan River Walk, a scenic stroll along the San Juan River in downtown Pagosa Springs, is dotted with sulfurous springs for smelling, soaking, and sightseeing. Pool sources range from underground hot springs to runoff from nearby commercial sites, and the conditions vary with the season and the weather. PHOTOS BY STEWART M. GREEN

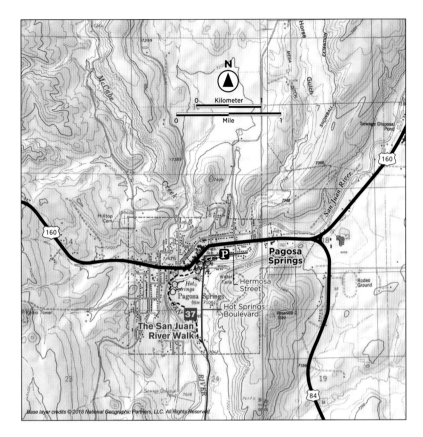

A few steps farther bring you to small pools left and right of the trail. Here you can scramble over rocks and boulders to the riverbank where several hot pools, suitable for soaking, await. Continue on the paved trail and keep an eye out for steam that directs you to more decorative springs to the right of the trail and hot soaking pools to the left.

Pass by the geodesic dome (part of the Geothermal Greenhouse Partnership) and past the community garden. At the edge of Centennial Park, cross another footbridge. In the distance ahead, the Mother Spring is in view on the grounds of The Springs Resort & Spa.

The paved trail crosses conservation wetlands, with more hot springs pools hidden in the tall grass. At the end of the trail, you can head back, or make a shorter loop of it by getting on Hot Springs Boulevard and walking north to Mary Fisher Park.

Area Highlights

Pagosa Springs is packed with hot springs, restaurants, and places to shop, but you can get your cultural fix here too.

The Pagosa Springs Center for the Arts hosts live shows by Thingamajig Theater Company, so check their site and pick up tickets before you go. From mid-May

Natural hot springs along the river walk vary from soaking pools to small fountains and large, steamy ponds. STEWART M. GREEN

to mid-September, you can view art and artifacts at the Fred Harman Western Art Museum and the San Juan Historical Museum.

Harman is best known as the creator of the *Red Ryder* comic strip, and every year, around Independence Day, Pagosa Springs is the site of the Red Ryder Roundup, featuring a parade and lots of activities.

38. TRIMBLE SPA & NATURAL HOT SPRINGS

Type: Family-oriented outdoor public and private swimming and soaking.

Location: Durango, about 70 west of Pagosa Springs.

When to visit: 7 days a week, except Wednesday in winter months, year-round.

Access: Year-round vehicle access on public roads. Call ahead for ADA access details.

Accommodations: 1-room guest-house for 2, and 2-bedroom guest-house for 5; RV park across the street, and motels nearby in Durango.

Rules: Day-soakers welcome. Clothing is required. No smoking, no alcohol, no glass, and no pets allowed.

Services: Full services in Durango.

Map & GPS: *DeLorme: Colorado Atlas & Gazetteer:* p. 86, A3; 37.391616 / -107.848337.

Contact: Trimble Spa & Natural Hot Springs, 6475 CR 203, Durango, CO 81301; (970) 247-0111; trimblehotsprings.com. Call or visit website for rates, reservations, and hours of operation.

How to get there: From Main Avenue in Durango, drive north on US 550 for about 9 miles and turn left onto CR 252 (Trimble Lane) and then right onto CR 203. From Ouray, take US 550 south for about 62 miles and turn right onto CR 252 (Trimble Lane) and then right onto CR 203. Trimble Hot Springs is on the left side of the road.

OVERVIEW

Trimble Spa & Natural Hot Springs provides the Durango community and out-of-town soakers with a lovely combination of outdoor swimming and soaking pools. There's an indoor sauna, massage and therapeutic treatment center, and picnic areas and lodging that invite romantic getaways, family outings, and special events. The open lawn with picnic tables, Adirondack chairs, a tent canopy, and leafy shade trees—with views of the San Juan Mountains—differentiate Trimble from other hot springs by giving visitors a place to set back away from the pool, lay out a blanket, and pop open a cooler for an experience that's as close to a day at the beach as you could hope for in Colorado.

The Hot Springs

Two large outdoor hot spring pools are filled with natural hot spring water maintained at 102° to 108°, depending on the season. The soaking pools are chemical-free. Nearby, the Olympic-sized swimming pool is 3 to 5 feet deep and surrounded by concrete decking. The water in this pool is not hot spring water but city-provided, chlorinated water that's heated by the hot springs to about 82°. A third soaking pool, the Red Rock Spa Pool, features whirlpool jets and is maintained at about 104°. This soaking pool does not contain hot spring water and is reserved for guests of the Starlight Room.

The Red Rock Spa Pool at Trimble Spa & Natural Hot Springs features whirlpool jets.
STEWART M. GREEN

The Site

The site design and lush greenery at Trimble Hot Springs present natural dividers between the varied offerings, providing subtle areas of privacy in a wide open space. There's a concession stand in the summer that's open from 11 a.m. to 3:30 p.m., plus long decks with great mountain views. Trimble allows outside food too— just leave the glass containers at home. Lounge chairs are available on a first-come, first-served basis, so grab one or feel free to bring your own. You may hear a train whistle while you're lying by the pool, as the Durango & Silverton Narrow Gauge Railroad passes by just across the highway to the east. Guests of the Starlight Room, a poolside, one-room guesthouse complete with a backyard patio and front porch with chairs, have private access to the whirlpool. The Starlight Room lends itself to romance, and, yes, Trimble Spa & Natural Hot Springs offers couples massages and more in its guest packages. For larger groups, there's the Trimble Guesthouse, with two bedrooms, one bathroom, and a fully equipped kitchen; call ahead for reservations. And if you're traveling through Durango in an RV, there's a park nearby with full hookups that will give you a discount on your visit to the hot springs. In addition to the pools, spa, and lodging, there are separate buildings on the premises housing a roomy dry sauna.

Trimble Spa & Natural Hot Springs provides the Durango community and visiting soakers with a lovely combination of outdoor swimming and soaking pools. STEWART M. GREEN

Hot Springs History

Over the years three hotels were raised and burned to the ground at Trimble Hot Springs. The first, built by Frank Trimble in 1882, burned just ten years later. A second hotel, Hermosa House, burned down in 1931. The third and last hotel to stand on the grounds included a dance floor, dining room, and enough glamour and style to attract the likes of Hollywood legends Clark Gable, Marilyn Monroe, Janet Leigh, and

Tony Curtis. This building also burned to the ground, and some believed the earth itself was cursed. When Ruedi Bear took ownership in 1957, he invited tribal leaders from the Southern Ute Tribe to the opening of the new Trimble Hot Springs, and they not only attended but blessed the grounds as well, ensuring a safe and fire-free future for the hot springs.

Area Highlights

Activities abound in Durango's high country, with plenty of great hiking, biking, and horseback riding trails in and around town. And if you left your pack, bike, or your horse at home, there are plenty of guide companies eager to serve you. Along with these side trips, plus nearby skiing and snowboarding at Durango Mountain Resort, two major attractions stand out as must-sees in this classic southwestern Colorado town. Hop on the Durango & Silverton Narrow Gauge Railroad for a breathtaking journey, all aboard a vintage steam engine on tracks that have been in service since 1882. The route travels right past Trimble Hot Springs and follows the Animas River for 45.4 miles in each direction, climbing almost 3,000 feet in elevation to the historic town of Silverton. Bring some cash for concessions and a camera—the train takes you through splendid canyons and wilderness with scenery usually reserved for only the most hard-core deep-country backpackers. In fact, the Durango & Silverton Narrow Gauge ferries mountain climbers to the trailhead of several 14,000-foot peaks, so don't be surprised to see hikers getting on and off the train with big packs and even bigger tales to tell of their mountaineering adventures in Chicago Basin, at the heart of the remote and spectacular Weminuche Wilderness Area. You'll cross the Animas River five times on the train from Durango to Silverton, but make time for a closer look with a rafting trip, kayaking, or even a zip-line tour over the river, through the woods, and with a prepared gourmet lunch in the treetops. If you overdo it out there, you can always come back to Trimble Spa & Natural Hot Springs for a spa treatment, a soak, or a long, restful nap under a shady tree.

39. PINKERTON HOT SPRINGS

Type: Outdoor public hot springs—not for soaking.

Location: Durango, about 70 miles west of Pagosa Springs.

When to visit: 7 days a week year-round.

Access: Year-round vehicle access on public roads. Hot spring is located at edge of a pullout, so ADA access is possible, depending on conditions.

Accommodations: None on-site, but tent and RV camping and motels are located in Durango.

Rules: No soaking.

Services: Full services in Durango.

Maps & GPS: *DeLorme: Colorado Atlas & Gazetteer:* p. 86, A3; *National Geographic Trails Illustrated #144,* Durango, Cortez; Hermosa Quadrangle. Parking and hot springs 37.451275 / -107.805234.

Contact: City of Durango, Natural Lands, Trails & Sustainability, (970) 375-7315, www.durangogov.org.

How to get there: From Main Avenue in Durango, take US 550 North for about 13 miles to a turnout on the right side of the road just past mile marker 35. There is a kiosk information board marking the location, and the hot springs are visible from the road.

OVERVIEW

Pinkerton Hot Springs is a whimsical roadside attraction and a lesson in what mineral water looks like when you remove the water. Situated feet from the highway north of Durango, if you blink, you'll miss it.

The Hot Springs

Hot spring water has minerals in it, and that's why we love it, but take out the water and what's left might amaze you, especially when it accumulates over time. Pinkerton Hot Springs is a steaming 8-foot-tall pile of mineral residue, basking in the sunshine and proudly displaying its deposits in brilliant swaths of reds, oranges, tans, and blacks. Water pours out from a spout on top, flows around the mound and onto the ground, then slips down the hillside to the Animas River.

The Site

The only development here is the big hot spring mineral pile itself, a parking area, and a small kiosk that explains the history of Pinkerton Hot Springs. If you get out of the car or have children with you, keep in mind that this is just feet from a national highway, so be sure to keep yourself and your kids off the road and away from the fast-moving vehicles.

Hot Springs History

Pinkerton Hot Springs originally sprouted from the west side of the highway, but when US 550 was repaved, the Colorado Department of Transportation laid a pipe to draw the water away from the road. A second, vertical pipe was added, surrounded by a pyramid of concrete blocks, so the redirected water could flow upward and downward, over the blocks, and down to the river. A turnout allowed for parking

Hot mineral water pours from a spout atop Pinkerton Hot Springs, and further north, another travertine flow can be spotted high on the hillside on the left side of the road. STEWART M. GREEN

so folks could pull off the road and safely view the spectacle. According to the kiosk, Pinkerton Hot Springs is named after La Plata County judge James Harvey Pinkerton. Judge Pinkerton was also a rancher and dairy farmer who—with the help of his wife and seven children—provided San Juan miners with dairy products in the late 1800s. Pinkerton built a bathhouse on the premises for hot spring soaking, and at one time the springs were bottled and sold as drinking water.

Area Highlights

Mesa Verde National Park is about a 1.5-hour drive from Pinkerton Hot Springs and makes for a fine day trip. Located near Cortez, Colorado, Mesa Verde protects more than 4,000 archaeological sites, including hundreds of well-preserved Anasazi cliff dwellings. Sites at Mesa Verde like Cliff Palace, the largest cliff dwelling in North America, were built into natural caves and beneath rocky ledges that jutted from the canyon walls, and served as homes, workplaces, and gathering spots for the Ancestral Pueblo people. High-pointers visiting Mesa Verde can get an easy summit on Park Point, the highest point of the park. Located atop a short paved trail, Park Point affords the casual hiker lovely views of the La Plata Mountains to the northeast, with peaks rising over 13,000 feet, including Hesperus Mountain, one of the four sacred peaks of the Dinétah, the original Navajo homeland.

40. **DUNTON HOT SPRINGS**

Type: Luxury-rustic public and private soaking, plus spa and massage services and lodging.

Location: Dolores, about 31 miles southwest of Telluride.

When to visit: 7 days a week year-round by reservation only.

Access: Year-round vehicle access on public roads. Call ahead for ADA access details.

Accommodations: 12 nineteenth-century cabins with private bathrooms; maximum capacity is 42 overnight guests.

Rules: No day-soakers. Pools are for guests only, and clothing is optional. Smoking permitted in certain designated outdoor areas. Pets allowed in some cabins with a daily surcharge.

Services: Full services are available 32 miles northeast in Telluride.

Map & GPS: *DeLorme: Colorado Atlas & Gazetteer*: p. 76, C1; 37.772493 / -108.092889.

Contact: Dunton Hot Springs, 52068 CR 38, Dolores, CO 81323; (970) 882-4800; http://duntonhotsprings.com. Call or visit website for rates, reservations, and hours of operation.

How to get there: From Denver, take US 285 South for 125 miles and turn right onto US 50 West. Drive 122 miles and then, in Montrose, follow signs to US 550 South. Drive 25 miles and turn right onto CO 62 West, then go 23 miles and turn left onto CO 145 South. Drive 30 miles and turn right onto Dunton Road. Continue about 10 miles to Dunton Hot Springs, on the left.

OVERVIEW

At first glance, Dunton Hot Springs is a deserted mining town left to decay in the high country. Cabins built in the 1800s cling to the landscape in a town left behind, a place where Butch Cassidy might have holed up after his first bank robbery, the one in Telluride back in 1889. But take a closer look and you'll find someone has breathed life into this ghost town and gently restored it to its nineteenth-century state while making it very, very comfortable. Dunton Hot Springs is what happens when old, quiet money meets the wild Old West. And if you mosey on into the saloon for a shot of Tennessee Dickel—the house whiskey—you'll see Butch Cassidy's name carved into the long wooden bar.

The Hot Springs

The hottest of the six tubs, baths, and pools is located at the source, where hot springs bubble up from the ground in an effervescent, 108° bath accessed by climbing down a ladder and into a deep tub. Behind the nineteenth-century bathhouse is an outdoor hot pool with views of the San Miguel Range. Inside, there's a large sunken pool, a hot shower, and a cold plunge bath for quick cooldowns. The fourth soaking option is an outdoor soaking pool outside the Dunton Store cabin, and the fifth hot spring is a truly natural experience, an undeveloped pool on the Dolores River. The sixth and final hot soak is a very old, rectangular copper tub reserved for guests of the Well House cabin. Hot spring water circulates through the developed pools every 4 hours, there is no

Each of the twelve cabins at Dunton Hot Springs is charming and unique in its own way.
SUSAN JOY PAUL

filtering or recirculation, and no chemicals are added. This is a clothing-optional facility, but swimsuits are certainly acceptable.

The Site

The twelve cabins at Dunton are all charming and unique in their own way. Over a century old, some still sit on the original spots where they were built, while others have been moved around a bit, and still others have been trucked in to replace those burned or otherwise destroyed by misuse. The owners have undertaken necessary improvements to make them comfortably habitable, but each one still retains most of the original structure. Additions to the decor include original art, antiques, and artifacts that blend and complement, rather than overwhelm, the museum-worthy interiors. They have not, thankfully, been unnecessarily fancied up, and this allows the original fixtures to shine through. The Echo Cabin has an outdoor shower, while the Well House has a hot springs–fed copper tub. There's a claw-foot bathtub in another cabin, with wheels added to the bottom so it could be rolled up the hill from its original home, a brothel that closed a long time ago. Most of the baths, and the new showers, too, have views of the surrounding wilderness, hillsides, and high peaks.

If you need to keep in touch with the outside world during your visit, there's Wi-Fi and a landline in each cabin, and video conferencing available in the dance hall. And if you think you're going to be roughing it, think again. Dunton Hot Springs has received numerous awards and kudos from travel aficionados, and articles in *Forbes* magazine and the *New York Times* extolled its design and luxuries. Movie stars, royalty, and businesspeople from around the world have enjoyed stays at Dunton, knowing this is not just a great place to get away and relax but also a place where the staff can provide you with whatever you want. Overnight stays at Dunton are all-inclusive, with gourmet meals served up in your cabin or family-style at the big table in the saloon. There are wines from around the world as well as from their own Sutcliffe Vineyard. Organically grown fruits and vegetables and local meats are prepared by a chef who can also whip up a picnic lunch for outdoor forays. In addition to the hot springs, mountain setting, library, spa, and one-of-a-kind accommodations, concierge services are prepared to attend to just about every outdoor adventure you can imagine, from ice climbing to hiking and heli-skiing, snowshoeing, rafting, and kayaking. Basically, if there's something you'd like to do, they can set it up for you. You can even rent the whole town for weddings, reunions, or a corporate retreat. Amid all the luxury, this is a very casual, comfortable place, with an engaging staff that will make you feel right at home.

Hot Springs History

The town of Dunton was established in 1885 as a row of cabins scattered along the West Dolores River. The mining camp was home to workers of the Emma, Smuggler, and American Mines. The town boomed around 1905 and went bust within a decade. From the 1970s through the 1980s, there was a dude ranch here, but squatters ran the place into the ground. In 1994 the current owners, Austrian developer and entrepreneur Bernt Kuhlmann and German businessman and heir to the Henkel International fortune Christoph Henkel, purchased the property and spent seven years restoring the cabins and, in 2001, Dunton Hot Springs was opened to the public.

The town of Dunton was established in 1885 as a row of cabins scattered along the West Dolores River; today it's home to Dunton Hot Springs, a high-end destination for soaking, glamping, and much more. SUSAN JOY PAUL

Area Highlights

The staff at Dunton Hot Springs can arrange all your San Juan adventures, but it's best to call ahead and make reservations to ensure them enough time for proper arrangements prior to your arrival. On other days you can enjoy slumming it in nearby Telluride. Situated in a box canyon, much of the town is listed on the National Register of Historic Places, and the surrounding high mountains and beautiful Ingram Falls serve as a perfect setting for the many festivals held here. The Telluride Film Festival attracts celebrity actors and filmmakers, while the Telluride Bluegrass Festival and Telluride Jazz Festival draw top musicians. There's a Telluride Blues & Brews Festival, a Telluride Chamber Music Festival, a Telluride Mushroom Festival, a Telluride Tech Festival, and plenty of other events to keep you dancing in the streets just about every weekend. In the wintertime you may just have to settle for skiing and snowboarding at Telluride's world-class ski resort, but you can give in to the slopes knowing that a massage, hot soak—and maybe a nap out in the hammock on the porch before supper—will be waiting for you back at Dunton Hot Springs.

Unique furnishings such as this old-fashioned claw-foot tub add to the charm at Dunton Hot Springs. SUSAN JOY PAUL

41. ORVIS HOT SPRINGS

Type: Cozy, quiet, indoor and outdoor public and private swimming and soaking, plus massage and lodging.

Location: Ridgway, about 28 miles south of Montrose.

When to visit: 7 days a week year-round.

Access: Year-round vehicle access on public roads. Call ahead for ADA access details.

Accommodations: 6 lodging rooms with shared baths and kitchen, tent pads, car camping, and some RV spots. No hookups.

Rules: Day-soakers welcome. Clothing is optional, except during the day at the indoor pool. No alcohol, glass, cameras, cell phones, or other electronic devices allowed. Smoking permitted at the Smoker's Pool, outdoor smoking area, and 1 guest room. Pets must be on leash at all times and are not allowed in the soaking area, on the grass, or in guest rooms.

Services: Full services in Ridgway.

Map & GPS: *DeLorme: Colorado Atlas & Gazetteer*: p. 66, D4; 38.134119 / -107.735400.

Contact: Orvis Hot Springs, 1585 CR 3, Ridgway, CO 81432; (970) 626-5324; www.orvishotsprings.com. Call or visit website for rates, reservations, and hours of operation.

How to get there: From Denver, take US 285 South for 125 miles and turn right onto US 50 West. Drive 122 miles and then, in Montrose, follow signs to US 550 South. Drive 27 miles and turn right onto CR 3. Orvis Hot Springs is on the right side of the road.

OVERVIEW

Some towns have a bar where folks gather to tell stories, exchange gossip, and catch up on the latest goings-on about town. For others, it's a cozy cafe where you can stop in to read the Sunday paper, maybe even do the crossword puzzle, get some help with it when you need it, and be left alone when you don't. Other towns have a barbershop where you can pull up a chair and join in the conversation. Like the song goes, it's that place "where everybody knows your name, and you're always glad you came." In Ridgway, that place is Orvis Hot Springs, and you don't have to be a regular to be welcomed into the fold.

The Hot Springs

Orvis Hot Springs features four outdoor soaking pools, a new Cold Plunge, an indoor soaking and swimming pool, and two private indoor tubs. Temperatures are adjusted for the season, ranging from 85° to 110° in the summertime and 100° to 114° in winter.

The largest outdoor pool, the Pond, is 40 feet wide and up to 5 feet deep at its center. The Pond is also a hot spring source, with waters bubbling up from the gravel bottom and seeping through rocky crevices, before settling in at 100° to 106°. This is a popular spot, with redwood decks, an adjoining cool plunge, and views of the Sneffels Range. Like all the outdoor pools at Orvis, it's protected with trees, shrubs, flowers, and carefully tended lawns and rock gardens. The second-largest outdoor pool is Island Pond, at 20 feet long, 8 feet wide, and 2 feet deep, while the Smoker's Pond

Enjoy views of the Sneffels Range at Orvis Hot Springs. STEWART M. GREEN

is about 8 feet round. Both of these pools have waterfalls and are 100° to 107°. As the name suggests, smoking is allowed in the Smoker's Pond. The Lobster Pot is the smallest and hottest pool, with temperatures from 108° to 114°. The outdoor pools are clothing-optional, and there's a dry sauna and yurts where you can enjoy a massage. The big swimming and soaking pool is 98°, and clothing is required by day.

You can bathe in privacy in two indoor soaking tubs. Wooden paneling surrounds each tub, and the baths are lined with tile and stone. There are big windows, too, where you can let in the sunshine and the mountain views. The private tubs are included with admission at Orvis, so you don't have to pay extra or reserve them; they're available on a first-come, first-served basis. All of the soaking options at Orvis are fed by two individual hot springs emerging at three locations on the grounds. No chemicals are added to the water.

The Site

The grounds at Orvis Hot Springs are meticulously maintained, and the lodge is just as neat and clean. Each of the six guest rooms follows a different theme. The Antique room features antique furniture and a skylight and is the only room where smoking is allowed. The Americana room has a handmade Amish bed; the Iron room, beds of iron; the Log Cabin room, beds of pine logs; and the Uncompahgre room has a big leather headboard. The Mount Sneffels room features a sleigh bed and views of the distinct and rugged Sneffels Range to the south. All rooms have free Wi-Fi and share two bathrooms with showers and a communal kitchen. If you prefer to camp out at Orvis, there's a gravel lot with wooden platforms and fire pits for tent camping, and space for car camping. RV spots are also available, but there are no hookups, and you must call in advance to reserve one. Overnight guests can use any of the soaking pools any time of day or night. Orvis Hot Springs has a team of massage therapists on staff that's practiced and certified in a number of styles and methodologies, including shiatsu, lomilomi, Watsu, Jin Shin Do, ashiatsu, and Trager. Call ahead for an appointment, just for yourself or to share with a friend.

Hot Springs History

Like many of Colorado's hot springs, Ute tribes gathered at Orvis to bathe in the waters many years ago. Lewis Orvis eventually took ownership of the property and completed a hot springs development that became a local gathering site. The property fell on hard times and into disrepair, but in 1987 Kim Goodman cleaned up the site and was instrumental in bringing it to its present state, currently managed by Mindy Kinsella.

Area Highlights

Ridgway's most famous denizen may be iconic fashion designer Ralph Lauren, who owns roughly 22,000 acres here, but movie actor Dennis Weaver also once called the town home. Weaver was a devoted humanitarian and environmentalist, and the Dennis Weaver Memorial Park celebrates his life with 60 acres along the Uncompahgre River. There you can visit the Eagle Memorial and Circle of Life, a monument that rises high, encircled by an astronomically aligned wheel of cairns. The park serves as a wildlife preserve and offers miles of hiking and biking trails, plus lots of grassy areas to lay a tablecloth and enjoy a picnic lunch.

For even more trails, and camping, too, head to Ridgway State Park. The park has three campgrounds, plus RV sites and yurts to rent, for overnight stays. There's boating, swimming, waterskiing, and sailboarding in the Ridgway Reservoir and Dallas Creek, and rafting and kayaking just south of the park, in the Uncompahgre River. Fourteen miles of trail are open to hiking and biking, and there are maps of it all at the visitor center.

Finally, Ridgway is surrounded by scenic drives. You can do the entire San Juan Skyway loop in about 6 hours or just do a piece of it; the Dallas Divide from Ridgway to Placerville, and Lizard Head Pass, between Ophir and Rico, are good choices. For a great detour, hit the dirt on Last Dollar Road—a 2-hour out-and-back that drops into Telluride—or drive over Owl Creek Pass in the Cimarron Mountains for spectacular views of Chimney Rock and Courthouse Mountain. This is the Colorado you see in old movies and new brochures: untouched, undeveloped, and unbelievable.

The big pool at Orvis Hot Springs is clothing-optional and cameras are not allowed.
COURTESY ORVIS HOT SPRINGS

42. TWIN PEAKS LODGE & HOT SPRINGS

Type: Family-oriented outdoor and indoor public swimming and soaking, plus lodging.

Location: Ouray, about 36 miles south of Montrose.

When to visit: 7 days a week year-round.

Access: Year-round vehicle access on public roads. Call ahead for ADA access details.

Accommodations: 54-room motel lodge, plus 15 private condos.

Rules: Day-soakers welcome. Clothing is required. Smoking in designated areas only. No glass. Pets may be accepted for motel guests, but call ahead for details.

Services: Full services in Ouray.

Map & GPS: *DeLorme: Colorado Atlas & Gazetteer:* p. 66, E4; 38.019128 / -107.673353.

Contact: Twin Peaks Lodge & Hot Springs, 125 3rd Ave., Ouray, CO 81427; (970) 325-4427; www.twin peakslodging.com. Call or visit website for rates, reservations, and hours of operation.

How to get there: From Denver, take US 285 South for 125 miles and turn right onto US 50 West. Drive 122 miles and then, in Montrose, follow signs to US 550 South. Drive 36 miles to downtown Ouray and turn right onto 3rd Avenue. Twin Peaks Hot Springs is on the left side of the road.

OVERVIEW

The town of Ouray is one of the loveliest in the state, a high alpine village surrounded by the mighty Sneffels Range. Lying on the south end of town, Twin Peaks Lodge & Hot Springs offers superb views of the mountains, while providing all the amenities you would expect from a large motel chain. If you like your hot springs served up with satellite television, Wi-Fi, and room service, then Twin Peaks may be your best choice. It's also a good option for family travelers, with a swimming pool, on-site restaurant, and rooms specially designed to accommodate kids.

The Hot Springs

You'll have three pools to pick from at Twin Peaks, and all are filled with fresh, hot mineral water. The large outdoor swimming pool is 5 feet deep in the middle and about 85°. There are lounge chairs, umbrella-shaded tables, and a clear windscreen to stave off the breezes while you enjoy the high-altitude sunshine. The outdoor soaking pool is about 105°. Both outdoor pools afford striking mountain views.

If you prefer your hot springs indoors and whirled, step into the bathhouse and enjoy a frothy soak in a sunken tub with jets, at about 107°. The Jacuzzi is open to motel guests 18 and older, 24 hours a day, and the soaking and swimming pools are open to all motel guests 24 hours a day.

The Site

The Twin Peaks Lodge & Hot Springs provides lodging with a fifty-four-room on-site motel, plus fifteen private condos located about 1.5 blocks away. The motel rooms come in a variety of configurations, from single king-bed rooms to double queen

You'll have three pools to pick from at Twin Peaks Lodge & Hot Springs, and all are filled with fresh, hot mineral water. The big swimming pool at Twin Peaks Lodge & Hot Springs features lounge chairs, umbrella-shaded tables, and a clear windscreen to stave off the breezes while you enjoy the high-altitude sunshine and mountain views. PHOTOS BY STEWART M. GREEN

rooms to family suites with bunk beds for kids ages 10 and younger. Condos have two and three bedrooms and two bathrooms. Rooms come with high-speed internet, refrigerators, and satellite TV, and guests have access to a 24-hour fitness center, laundry, and vending machines. There's a breakfast room where lodgers can enjoy a free hot breakfast every morning, and a restaurant that serves pizza, sandwiches, salad, and more. Outside is a grassy picnic area and shuffleboard for daytime use, and on summer evenings you can visit the open-air tiki bar for beer and mixed drinks. The downtown area is just a block away, and if you'd like to venture a little farther, the concierge service can arrange for a Jeep rental or set you up with a guide for a number of other Rocky Mountain high adventures.

Hot Springs History

Twin Peaks Lodge sits on the foundation of a residence built in 1893 by Alf Armstrong, one of the three founders of the Bachelor Mine. The home was purchased by Eugene and Velma Tankersley in 1960, and in 1978 the business—then known as Twin Peaks Motel—and property were sold to Robert and Sylvia Madura. The Tankersleys and the Maduras made numerous improvements to the site, including replacing the home's garage with an A-frame structure that now serves as the office and front desk of the Twin Peaks Lodge. Outdoor pools were dug, the lodge was expanded, a structure was erected to house the indoor soaking pool, and many aesthetic touches were added.

Area Highlights

Ouray is chock-full of more activities than you will ever have days to enjoy them, so choose your adventure and make the most of your time here. There's hiking, biking, and rock climbing in the summer, and ice climbing, Nordic skiing, and snowshoeing in the winter. World-famous Telluride Ski Resort is about an hour away, and the Twin Peaks concierge service can arrange a shuttle for you. If you're visiting in the summer months, they can also arrange for a Jeep rental so you can discover some of Colorado's most scenic four-wheel-drive roads on your own. If you're new to four-wheeling, consider a trip on Last Dollar Road to Telluride; the drive features views of the Sneffels Range and lots of colorful trees for autumn "leaf-peeping." In the summertime enjoy the wildflowers with a drive into Yankee Boy Basin, where you'll end up at the base of 14,150-foot Mount Sneffels and majestic 13,694-foot Gilpin Peak. For a slightly more challenging drive, head up Corkscrew Gulch and top out at 12,217 feet before dropping into the Cement Creek Drainage; from there, choose your route down to Silverton or up to Hurricane Pass. Whatever route you choose, be sure to know both your limits and your vehicle's limits, stick to the roads, and take your time. The slower you go, the more you'll see, and the more you'll have to talk about in the whirlpool tub or at the tiki bar back at the Twin Peaks Lodge.

43. BOX CANYON LODGE & HOT SPRINGS

Type: Cozy, quiet outdoor public soaking, plus lodging.

Location: Ouray, about 36 miles south of Montrose.

When to visit: 7 days a week year-round.

Access: Year-round vehicle access on public roads. Call ahead for ADA access details.

Accommodations: 3 motel lodges comprising 39 units, including a 2-bedroom, 2-bath apartment and many king bed, queen bed, and combination suites.

Rules: No day-soakers; hot tubs are for lodging guests only. Clothing is required. No smoking, no pets.

Services: Full services in Ouray.

Map & GPS: *DeLorme: Colorado Atlas & Gazetteer:* p. 66, E4; 38.019054 / -107.674710.

Contact: Box Canyon Lodge & Hot Springs, 45 3rd Ave., Ouray, CO 81427; (970) 325-4981; www.box canyonouray.com. Call or visit website for rates, reservations, and hours of operation.

How to get there: From Denver, take US 285 South for 125 miles and turn right onto US 50 West. Drive 122 miles and then, in Montrose, follow signs to US 550 South. Drive 36 miles to downtown Ouray and turn right onto 3rd Avenue. Box Canyon Hot Springs is on the left side of the road.

OVERVIEW

Box Canyon Lodge & Hot Springs is unique, with outdoor hot spring tubs built into the landings of a redwood deck that climbs the canyon, culminating in a wooden platform for sunning. As you leave the sundeck, you find yourself high on a hillside with bench seats and swings. From this vantage point, you are treated to views of the town below and mountaintops all around. Ouray is known as the "Switzerland of America," and from your grassy perch, surrounded by 13,000-foot peaks, you may be tempted to break out into an impromptu rendition of "The Sound of Music." It's just that pretty.

The Hot Springs

Although the hot springs sprout from the earth at 140°, the four outdoor jetted tubs are maintained at a pleasant 101° to 108° and covered while not in use to keep them hot and clean. The water is replaced every 24 hours, and there is no chlorine or other chemicals added. The redwood decking is tiered and interspersed with leafy trees, providing soakers with a semblance of privacy between tubs, while allowing everyone a view of the surrounding peaks and sky. The area is clean and well maintained, the kind of place you would be proud to bring a friend or partner.

The Site

Box Canyon Lodge & Hot Springs enjoys an ideal location in Ouray; shopping and restaurants are less than 2 blocks to the east, while the Ouray Ice Park lies to the west. In fact, the ice-climbing area known as Gazebo Wall is a mere 5-minute walk from the front door of the lodge. There are thirty-nine units in the lodge in several

configurations to suit any number of guests, from individuals to couples, families, or small groups. Each room is well appointed, with pine tongue-in-groove paneling, marble countertops, and air-conditioning, and they all include a microwave oven, refrigerator, coffeemaker, hair dryer, free Wi-Fi, and satellite TV. Long decks surround the rooms at the lodge and make a good place to enjoy a cup of coffee in the morning, and in the summertime you can also enjoy the sweet smell of ivy geraniums that spill out of the window boxes. In recent years the owners at Box Canyon Lodge & Hot Springs have adopted a green initiative, effectively reducing their gas consumption by 70 percent. Guest rooms and indoor water are now heated with the geothermal waters of the hot springs, and a number of other changes at the lodge have earned it a four-key rating from eco-rating program Green Key.

Hot Springs History

Utes frequented the hot springs in Box Canyon long before the first trappers and prospectors moved into the area. In 1925 Bessi and Richard Cogar built the Cogar Sanitarium and in 1929 sold it to Charles Kent, who renamed it the Sweet Skin Sanitarium. The property moved through several more owners and developed into the lodge that rests on part of the Cogars' original acreage. In 2005 Rich and Karen Avery took over the Box Canyon Lodge & Hot Springs and have since made a number of subtle but welcome improvements, such as replacing the hot tubs, adding a laundry for guests, and building bench swings and seats at the top of the tiered terrace area where you can enjoy the solitude and views.

Area Highlights

With miles of summertime hiking and biking trails and hundreds of rock-climbing routes, along with winter access to snowshoeing and Nordic skiing and a world-class ice-climbing park, the choices here are nearly endless. If you like scenic drives, Camp Bird Road will take you up to the Camp Bird Mine, where you should park, as the road beyond isn't safe for passenger cars. You can get out and hike up to Yankee Boy Basin, where in the summertime you'll be treated to fields of wildflowers and great views of fourteener Mount Sneffels, and thirteener Mount Gilpin. If you carry a backpack, bring along a tablecloth and a picnic lunch and make an afternoon of it. Or take a drive up to Owl Creek Pass and be on the lookout for wildlife, as well as locations for scenes from *True Grit*, as this is where that John Wayne movie was filmed. Just before you gain the pass, note the meadow on the

Facing page: Soaking tubs are reserved for overnight guests only at Box Canyon Lodge & Hot Springs. Above: You can visit the source of steamy waters at Box Canyon Lodge & Hot Springs. PHOTOS BY STEWART M. GREEN

The Sneffels Range surrounds Ouray and soakers at Box Canyon Lodge & Hot Springs.
STEWART M. GREEN

left side of the road, where the Duke and his nemeses engaged in a wild shootout at that film's end.

For hiking, the Box Canyon Falls Trail will take you into the canyon and provide spectacular views of the falls, and if you go in the summertime and have to pay a fee for access, you won't regret the small cost. For a longer hike, check out the Portland Trail, which starts at the Amphitheater Campground and meanders up and down through the basin. Finally, Baby Bathtubs is a terrific hike for young children—short and scenic, you can do it in under an hour, and then see if they're up for something a bit longer. If you visit the Box Canyon Lodge & Hot Springs in wintertime, you can enjoy all these trails on snowshoes or cross-country skis, or head to Ironton Park for marked and groomed trails and a look at a historic ghost town. After a full day in Ouray, you can always head back to Box Canyon Lodge & Hot Springs for a hot shower, hot soak, and a hot meal at one of the town's many restaurants. You'll have plenty to talk about over dinner!

44. THE HISTORIC WIESBADEN HOT SPRINGS SPA & LODGINGS

Type: Cozy, quiet outdoor and indoor public soaking, swimming, and vapor caves, plus massage and spa services and lodging.

Location: Ouray, about 36 miles south of Montrose.

When to visit: 7 days a week year-round. Call ahead for holidays.

Access: Year-round vehicle access on public roads. Call ahead for ADA access details.

Accommodations: 17-room lodge and large rental house; one pet-friendly unit on Main Street, 2 blocks from the main lodge.

Rules: Day-soakers welcome. Clothing is required in swimming pool and vapor cave, but optional in the private soaking pool. No smoking, no smokers, and no exceptions. No glass containers and no pets allowed around pools or in cave.

Services: Full services in Ouray.

Map & GPS: *DeLorme: Colorado Atlas & Gazetteer:* p. 66, E4; 38.023027 / -107.668465.

Contact: Wiesbaden Hot Springs Spa & Lodgings, 625 5th St., Ouray, CO 81427; (970) 325-4347; www .wiesbadenhotsprings.com. Call or visit website for rates, reservations, and hours of operation.

How to get there: From Denver, take US 285 South for 125 miles and turn right onto US 50 West. Drive 122 miles and then, in Montrose, follow signs to US 550 South. Drive 36 miles to downtown Ouray and turn left onto 6th Avenue and left again onto 5th Street. The Wiesbaden is on the right side of the road.

OVERVIEW

The town of Ouray, built on steep roads at the entrance to a narrow valley amid high mountain peaks, displays a distinct European influence with Victorian antiquity and architecture. Nowhere is this more evident than The Historic Wiesbaden Hot Springs Spa & Lodgings, the oldest commercial spring in a town nearly bursting with hot springs. The Wiesbaden echoes early American splendor and old-world charm, harking back to a more peaceful time of relaxation and quiet reflection. It's like a big overstuffed chair that you sink into and may never want to leave.

The Hot Springs

All three soaking options offer pure, fresh hot spring water with no chlorine or other additives. The outdoor swimming pool is maintained at 100° to 105°, depending on the season. There are tables and chairs for sitting, lounge chairs for sunning, and shade trees that provide a cool respite from the Colorado sunshine if needed. Children under 6 are not allowed in the pool, but a plastic kiddie pool that can be filled with hot spring water and placed alongside the swimming pool is provided on request.

A second option is the vapor cave. Carved into bedrock, the cave's first chamber features a warm 78° spring that spouts from the rock. In the main chamber, a second hot spring enters the cave from below the ground at 121°, creating a steamy

The Historic Wiesbaden Hot Springs Spa & Lodgings echoes early American splendor and old-world charm. STEWART M. GREEN

compartment and filling a shallow soaking pool with 107° to 109° water. The caves are power-washed regularly to remove outside contaminants, and no chemicals are used. Overnight guests of the Wiesbaden have complimentary access to the vapor cave and the swimming pool and are allowed extended hours. Both are available to day-soakers for a fee.

The third soaking option is an outdoor private soaking pool, the Lorelei. Situated in an enclosed area beside a hot spring waterfall and beneath the white blossoms of an apple tree, the Lorelei is cast of stone, and the waters range from 102° to 105°. With shady trees, a waterfall, and crystal waters interrupted only occasionally by a creamy white apple blossom, the Lorelei lends itself to couples soaks. It's available to lodge guests and day-soakers, at an hourly rate.

The Site

The seventeen-room lodge at the Wiesbaden is bordered by a wooden deck that's lined with long benches and patio chairs, and looks out onto a grassy lawn with more seating and shade trees, the perfect place for curling up for a few hours with a good book. The rooms are mountain-town perfect, with white linen curtains, quilted bedding, and pedestal sinks and vanities. Each has a telephone and television, and you'll appreciate the landlines, as some cell phone carriers do not provide service in Ouray. There are other Wiesbaden rental properties available, too—cottages and houses—so if you're traveling with a large group, you may want to inquire ahead as to their availability.

The lobby at the Wiesbaden is warm and filled with light, even in the winter months, due to its cathedral ceiling, skylights, comfy couches, pillows, and a bounty

One of three soaking options at The Historic Wiesbaden Hot Springs Spa & Lodgings, the Lorelei is a private, enclosed soaking pool. STEWART M. GREEN

of green plants. Downstairs, Veda Spa offers all sorts of massage, spa, and reflexology treatments. The massage tables are set in rooms with walls of intricate masonry and sheer rock face, and vapor cave treatments are available on request. Like all the hot springs of Ouray, the Wiesbaden enjoys impressive mountain views. To the south, 12,801-foot Abrams Mountain dominates the skyline, while carved in the cliffs to the east stands the cirque-shaped Amphitheater.

Hot Springs History

The commercial hot springs at Wiesbaden date back to 1832, when Ouray postmaster and apothecary A. G. Dunbarton discovered a forty-barrel-per-hour flow of hot water while building his house on the site. He constructed Dunbarton's Plunge Bathhouse, then bought another site, built a two-story structure, and piped in more hot water. During the Great Depression, Dunbarton's properties were sold, then sold again. The larger of the developments became the Ouray Mineral Hot Springs. In 1926 the properties were sold to Dr. Charles V. Bates, who excavated the vapor caves and ran a hospital, the Radium Vapor Health Institute, for nearly twenty years. That structure is now the Ouray County Historical Museum. Linda Wright-Minter purchased the property in 1978.

Area Highlights

Ouray is a veritable playground for the Colorado adventurer, boasting miles of hiking and biking trails, a world-class ice-climbing park, rock climbing, and access to snowshoeing, Nordic skiing, and of course, Telluride. If you like scenic drives, there are plenty of them in the area. Head north for the Dallas Divide, a high pass between the San Miguel and Uncompahgre Rivers. The drive—from Ouray north on CO 550 to Ridgway and then west on CO 62, and southeast on CO 145 to Telluride—offers stunning views of 14,000-foot peaks Uncompahgre and Wetterhorn to the east, while passing close by Mount Sneffels, another Colorado fourteener, to the south. Or go south on CO 550 from Ouray, and tour the stretch of road to Silverton known as the Million Dollar Highway. Allow plenty of time for each drive, as the roads can twist and turn, rise up sharply, and drop just as quickly; bring a camera and be sure to pull over now and then to enjoy the views. If you'd like to stretch your legs in Ouray, there are lots of hikes that can be done in an hour, offering spectacular views of the area. The Lower Cascade Falls Trail is short, sweet, and steep, but your reward is a waterfall at the end! Or choose the Ice Park Trail. From the trailhead at Camp Bird Mine Road, the hike follows a gorge on one side, crosses a river, and returns on the other side. For a longer day, you can opt for the Ouray Perimeter Trail, a roughly 5-mile loop that begins at the Ouray Visitors Center and circles the entire town, with fantastic views of 13,000-foot peaks, Uncompahgre Gorge, and the Amphitheater. Wherever you go, and however you get there, the hot springs and vapor caves will be waiting for you back at the Wiesbaden.

45. OURAY HOT SPRINGS POOL & FITNESS CENTER

Type: Family-oriented outdoor public swimming and soaking, plus fitness center.

Location: Ouray, about 36 miles south of Montrose.

When to visit: 7 days a week year-round.

Access: Year-round vehicle access on public roads. ADA access to changing rooms, pool area, and into most pools via ramps. Hydraulic chair-to-pool lift and submersible chair.

Accommodations: None on-site, but tent and RV camping and motels are located in and around Ouray.

Rules: Day-soaker facility. Clothing is required. No smoking, no alcohol, and no glass containers. No food in the pool. Service animals only.

Services: Full services in Ouray.

Map & GPS: *DeLorme: Colorado Atlas & Gazetteer:* p. 66, E4; 38.028836 / -107.672845.

Contact: Ouray Hot Springs Pool & Fitness Center, 1220 Main St., Ouray, CO 81427; (970) 325-7073; http://ourayhotsprings.com. Call or visit website for rates and hours of operation.

How to get there: From Montrose, follow signs to US 550 South. Drive 35 miles to the town of Ouray. The Ouray Hot Springs Pool & Fitness Center is located on the right side of the road on the north end of town.

OVERVIEW

It's hard to imagine a better location for a big hot spring pool than the town of Ouray. After a long day of ice climbing in Box Canyon, biking the Portland Trail, climbing at Rotary Park, or scrambling to the top of 14,150-foot Mount Sneffels, the big pool at Ouray is divine salvation. If you make Ouray your home base for any of these activities, the Ouray Hot Springs Pool & Fitness Center is a good choice to soothe those sore muscles and let the intensity of the day's activities drift away.

The Hot Springs

The water here is 156° at the source, and the pools vary from 78° to 106°. The entire pool area was renovated and reopened in the spring of 2017. The big pool is 250 feet long by 150 feet wide and contains over a million gallons of water. It's partitioned into five sections that separately accommodate swimming, soaking, and water play. One of the sections is perfect for soaking: Located at the east end of the pool, it's 2 to 3.5 feet deep and a steamy 102° to 106°. There are two sections, reserved for children and non-swimmers, that are about 4 feet deep and 91° to 95°. Other sections of the pool range from 5 to 9 feet deep and include lap lanes, a diving area, and a game area for water volleyball and basketball. The pool also has two slides, and there are always lifeguards on duty, but children under 6 years of age still must have an adult within reach at all times.

The Ouray Hot Springs Pool is fed from water from nearby Box Canyon Hot Springs and supplemented by two 90-foot-deep wells. The waters are kept algae-free between cleanings with chlorine. There is a large pump room on the property where

Top: The pool area at Ouray Hot Springs Pool & Fitness Center is partitioned into five sections for swimming, soaking, and water play. Bottom: Catch some rays or shade in the hot soaking pools at Ouray Hot Springs Pool & Fitness Center. PHOTOS BY STEWART M. GREEN

excess iron is filtered from the incoming water, which is then treated and the temperature adjusted through a complex valve system before being diverted to various sections of the pool. As with any hot spring pool this size, the care and maintenance that go into ensuring a good experience for patrons are a lot more complicated than you might imagine.

The Site
The Ouray Hot Springs Pool features a playground; an on-site, food-truck-style snack bar and grill; and a fitness center complete with free weights, machines, and cardio equipment. There's an in-pool rock wall and an obstacle course, too.

The big park next to Ouray Hot Springs Pool has picnic tables, barbecue grills, a playground, running track, softball diamond, basketball courts, horseshoe pits, a skate park, an event space for parties, and lots of room for just running around in the grass.

Hot Springs History
The natural waters that feed the Ouray Pool were reined in due to efforts by the Ouray Recreation Association Corporation, and the pool was built in 1927 to provide the local community with swimming and soaking, and to attract more tourism to Ouray. The July 4 opening drew the largest crowd ever gathered in the town. Now owned by the City of Ouray, the site continues to be a favorite among locals, a popular attraction for tourists, and a welcome respite for weary high-country adventurers. Recent renovations include sparkling white pool bottoms and wraparound underwater seating. Rumor has it that the bathhouses will soon be remodeled.

Area Highlights
Ouray is the ice-climbing capital of North America. The world's first ice-climbing park was developed on Ouray's southwest edge in the Uncompahgre Gorge by supplementing existing, natural falls with dozens of farmed waterfalls. The sprinkler system feeding the frozen falls covers a distance of more than a mile, creating walls of ice that rise 80 to 200 feet from the gorge floor. The Ouray Ice Park is free to visitors, since the development and upkeep of its infrastructure are made possible by volunteers and donations from area businesses, gear companies, and benevolent climbers. The annual weeklong Ouray Ice Festival is the largest event of its kind in North America, drawing crowds from around the world and offering opportunities to enjoy a variety of clinics, presentations, and gear demonstrations. If this is your first time on ice, or if you're just looking to improve your kicks and swings or add to your technical climbing skills, there are guide services and gear shops in Ouray that can rent or sell you the necessary gear and provide you with the instruction and guidance you need to stay safe.

While the rock climbing in Ouray may not be as sweet as the ice, there are plenty of local crags where you can practice your sport-climbing moves; Rotary Park, Pool Wall, the Sandias, and Rock Park offer hundreds of routes. A visit to Ouray may be the perfect opportunity to try out a new sport, or revisit an old one, and there's plenty of water in the big Ouray Hot Springs Pool to gently melt away whatever pings, pangs, bruises, and bangs you suffer in your extreme rock and ice adventures.

APPENDIX A: GPS COORDINATES OF ALL COLORADO HOT SPRINGS

According to the National Oceanic and Atmospheric Administration (NOAA) and the National Centers for Environmental Information (NCEI), 1,661 thermal springs are known to exist in the United States, and 47 are in Colorado. This includes warm (below body temperature), hot, and boiling springs. Each entry in the list below includes the latitude, longitude, USGS spring name, maximum surface temperature, Army Map Service (AMS) map name, and United States Geological Survey (USGS) quadrangle map name of these Colorado hot springs.

Many commercial hot springs facilities use a name other than the USGS name, so without tracking them down by coordinates, it's sometimes impossible to associate the two. Even then, a hot spring facility may be located far from the actual hot spring source, such as Salida Hot Springs Aquatic Center, where the hot spring water is piped in from mountains around Poncha Springs, miles to the west. Also, a single hot spring can emanate from several locations, and so one hot spring listed below may appear as two or many more at a facility. For example, Hot Sulphur Springs is listed just once below, but there are seven individual hot springs in that area, all emanating from the same source. Likewise, Orvis Hot Springs has two hot springs, but one of them reaches the surface at two locations on the property, for a total of three hot springs from two sources.

Since the term *hot spring* is used interchangeably to describe the hot spring at the source below ground and the hot spring as it surfaces, it's easy to confuse the data and hard to get an accurate count. Also, as the data in this list is from 1980 and there is no known survey available with later results, it's possible that some of these hot springs may have dried up since this report was created, and also that new hot springs have appeared. Finally, the temperatures of hot springs can change over time, and the Fahrenheit number shown below may not be up-to-date. Temperatures provided for each hot spring in the chapters of this book have been measured more recently and thus tend to be more accurate.

GPS	Hot Spring	Temperature	AMS, USGS Map
38.7320 / -106.178	Hortense Hot Spring	181	Montrose, Poncha Springs 15
38.5140 / -106.508	Upper Waunita Hot Springs	176	Montrose, Pitkin 7.5
38.5170 / -106.515	Lower Waunita Hot Springs	167	Montrose, Pitkin 7.5
38.4980 / -106.076	Poncha Hot Springs	160	Montrose, Bonanza 15
38.0210 / -107.672	Ouray Hot Springs	156	Montrose, Ouray 7.5
40.5590 / -106.849	Routt Hot Springs	147	Craig, Rocky Peak 7.5
38.1680 / -105.924	Mineral Hot Springs	140	Pueblo, Villa Grove 7.5
38.8120 / -106.226	Cottonwood Hot Springs	136	Montrose, Buena Vista 15

Facing page: Soakers enjoy the creekside pools at Mount Princeton.
STEWART M. GREEN

37.2630 / -107.011	Pagosa Springs	136	Durango, Pagosa Springs 7.5
37.7470 / -106.831	Wagon Wheel Gap Hot Springs	135	Durango, Spar City 15
38.7330 / -106.162	Mount Princeton Hot Springs	133	Montrose, Poncha Springs 15
39.2270 / -107.224	Penny Hot Springs	133	Leadville, Redstone 7.5
39.0170 / -105.793	Hartsel Hot Springs	126	Denver, Hartsel 7.5
38.1330 / -107.736	Orvis Hot Spring	126	Montrose, Dallas 7.5
39.5480 / -107.322	Glenwood Springs	124	Leadville, Glenwood Springs 7.5
39.5520 / -107.412	South Canyon Hot Springs	118	Leadville, Storm King Mountain 7.5
39.7390 / -105.512	Idaho Springs	115	Denver, Idaho Springs 7.5
37.7520 / -108.131	Paradise Warm Spring	115	Cortez, Groundhog Mountain 7.5
40.0730 / -106.113	Hot Sulphur Springs	111	Craig, Hot Sulphur Springs 15
37.4000 / -107.849	Tripp Hot Springs	111	Durango, Hermosa 7.5
37.7710 / -108.091	Dunton Hot Spring	108	Cortez, Dolores Peak 7.5
37.3130 / -107.344	Piedra River Hot Springs	108	Durango, Devil Mountain 7.5
38.2720 / -107.100	Cebolla Hot Springs	106	Montrose, Powderhorn 7.5
38.4330 / -105.261	Cañon City Hot Springs	104	Pueblo, Royal Gorge 15
37.5110 / -106.945	Rainbow Hot Springs	104	Durango, Spar City 15
40.4830 / -106.827	Steamboat Springs	102	Craig, Steamboat Springs 7.5
39.0120 / -106.891	Conundrum Hot Springs	100	Leadville, Maroon Bells 7.5
40.4670 / -107.952	Juniper Hot Springs	100	Craig, Juniper Hot Springs 7.5
38.1920 / -105.816	Valley View Hot Springs	99	Pueblo, Valley View Hot Springs 7.5
37.3910 / -107.846	(Trimble) Stratten Warm Spring	97	Durango, Hermosa 7.5
38.0140 / -108.054	Lemon Hot Spring	91	Moab, Placerville 7.5
38.4850 / -105.910	Wellsville Warm Spring	91	Pueblo, Howard 15
37.7410 / -107.034	Antelope Spring	90	Durango, Workman Creek 7.5
39.6280 / -107.106	Dotsero Warm Springs	90	Leadville, Glenwood Springs 15
37.4530 / -107.803	Pinkerton Hot Springs	90	Durango, Hermosa 7.5
37.7280 / -107.054	Birdsie Warm Spring	86	Durango, Workman Creek 7.5
37.7510 / -106.317	Shaw Springs	86	Durango, Twin Mountains SE 7.5
37.7470 / -108.117	Geyser Warm Spring	82	Cortez, Rico 7.5
38.4790 / -105.891	Swissvale Warm Springs	82	Pueblo, Howard 15
38.8160 / -106.873	Ranger Hot Spring	81	Montrose, Cement Mountain 7.5
37.0330 / -106.805	Stinking Springs	81	Durango, Chromo 15
39.9320 / -105.277	Eldorado Springs	79	Denver, Eldorado Springs 7.5
38.6530 / -106.056	Browns Canyon Warm Spring	77	Montrose, Poncha Springs 15
38.8360 / -106.825	Cement Creek Hot Spring	77	Montrose, Cement Mountain 7.5
39.1640 / -106.062	Rhodes Warm Spring	75	Leadville, Fairplay West 7.5
38.6340 / -106.072	Browns Grotto Warm Spring	73	Montrose, Poncha Springs 15
37.2940 / -105.784	Dexter Spring	68	Trinidad, Pikes Stockade 7.5

APPENDIX B: MINERAL CONTENT OF THE HOT SPRINGS

Some commercial hot springs publish the mineral content of their water; available information is listed below. For most, quantities are shown as "mg/L" (milligrams per liter) and "µg/L" (micrograms per liter). A milligram is 1/1,000th of a gram, and a microgram is 1/1,000th of a milligram. When measurements are given in parts per million (ppm) and parts per billion (ppb), assume that ppm = (approximately) mg/L, or milligrams per liter, and ppb = (approximately) µg/L, or micrograms per liter. Grains per gallon are listed as "gr.gal."

ANTERO HOT SPRING CABINS
Sodium 61 mg/L; sulfate 60 mg/L; silica 53 mg/L; calcium 8.3 mg/L; chloride 4.9 mg/L; potassium 2.1 mg/L; nitrogen 0.15 mg/L; lithium 100 µg /L; iron 50 µg /L; boron 20 µg /L; zinc 20 µg /L; fluoride 10 µg /L; arsenic 1 µg /L; magnesium 0.3 µg /L; manganese 0 µg /L.

AVALANCHE RANCH CABINS & HOT SPRINGS
Sulfate 930 mg/L; sodium 323 mg/L; calcium 287 mg/L; chloride 230 mg/L; magnesium 29.5 mg/L; potassium 28.1 mg/L; fluoride 2.4 mg/L; iron 1.1 mg/L; lithium 0.935 mg/L; manganese 0.935 mg/L; zinc 0.00535 mg/L; barium 0.0296 mg/L; arsenic 0.00405 mg/L; selenium 0.00313 mg/L.

BLACK SULPHUR SPRING
Alkalinity 2,218 mg/L; bicarbonate 2,218 mg/L; sodium, dissolved 1940 mg/L; chloride 1,230 mg/L; sulfate 574 mg/L; hardness 237 mg/L; potassium, dissolved 110 mg/L; calcium, dissolved 49 mg/L; magnesium, dissolved 28 mg/L; fluoride 3.3 mg/L; lithium, dissolved 2.75 mg/L; iron, dissolved 0.39 mg/L; barium, dissolved 0.03 mg/L; arsenic, dissolved 0.027 mg/L.

BOX CANYON LODGE & HOT SPRINGS
Sulfate 1,130.0000 mg/L; calcium 336.0000 mg/L; bicarbonate 127.0000 mg/L; sodium 124.0000 mg/L; chloride 41.0000 mg/L; magnesium 19.0000 mg/L; potassium 16.6000 mg/L; nitrate 6.0300 mg/L; fluoride 2.2500 mg/L; manganese 0.6260 mg/L; boron 0.6220 mg/L; iron 0.3100 mg/L; barium 0.0300 mg/L; phosphate 0.0250 mg/L; arsenic 0.0160 mg/L; molybdenum 0.0080 mg/L; zinc 0.0050 mg/L; selenium 0.0030 mg/L; lead 0.0010 mg/L; cadmium 0.0002 mg/L; chromium 0.0000 mg/L; copper 0.0000 mg/L; mercury 0.0000 mg/L; silver 0.0000 mg/L.

COTTONWOOD HOT SPRINGS INN & SPA
Sulfate 110 mg/L; sodium 105 mg/L; silica 57 mg/L; chloride 30 mg/L; calcium 5.9 mg/L; potassium 2.7 mg/L; nitrogen 0.12 mg/L; lithium 155 µg /L; boron 92.5 µg /L; zinc 15 µg /L; fluoride 14 µg /L; iron 10 µg /L; manganese 10 µg /L; arsenic 4.5 µg /L; magnesium 0.4 µg /L.

GLENWOOD HOT SPRINGS RESORT

Chloride 11,000 mg/L; sodium 6,900 mg/L; sulfate 1,100 mg/L; calcium 510 mg/L; potassium 180 mg/L; magnesium 91 mg/L; fluoride 2.3 mg/L; phosphate—ortho 0.12 mg/L, ortho diss, as P 0.04 mg/L; nitrogen 0.01 mg/L; boron 890 µg /L; lithium 800 µg /L; manganese 80 µg /L; iron 60 µg /L; silica 32 µg /L; zinc 30 µg /L.

HEALING WATERS RESORT & SPA

Total solids 3,348.8 ppm (195.3 gr.gal.); organic and volatile matter 252.0 ppm (14.7 gr.gal.); sulfated residue 3,617.6 ppm (211.0 gr.gal.); silica 44.1 ppm (2.6 gr.gal.); iron and alumina oxides 5.3 ppm (0.3 gr.gal.); lime 339.6 ppm (19.8 gr.gal.); magnesia 42.6 ppm (2.5 gr.gal.); chloride 139.5 ppm (8.1 gr.gal.); bicarbonate 482.0 ppm (28.1 gr. gal.); sulfate 1,590.4 ppm (92.8 gr.gal.); sodium oxide 1,142.6 ppm (66.6 gr.gal.).

HEART SPRING

Sodium, dissolved 300 mg/L; alkalinity 183 mg/L; sulfate 150 mg/L; bicarbonate 103 mg/L; chloride 320 mg/L; carbonate 84 mg/L; hardness 49 mg/L; silica 49 mg/L; calcium, dissolved 18 mg/L; magnesium, dissolved 1 mg/L; potassium, dissolved 11 mg/L; fluoride 1.9 mg/L; boron 0.7 mg/L; lithium, dissolved 0.35 mg/L; iron, dissolved 0.04 mg/L; nitrogen 0.04 mg/L, arsenic, dissolved 0.005 mg/L.

HOT SULPHUR SPRINGS RESORT & SPA

Sodium 435 mg/L; chloride 145 mg/L; sulfate 145 mg/L; silica 33 mg/L; potassium 24 mg/L; calcium 15 mg/L; fluoride 11 mg/L; magnesium 3.2 mg/L; lithium 1.3 mg/L; trace elements of iron, manganese, and zinc.

INDIAN HOT SPRINGS

Sodium 520 ppm; sulfate 420 ppm; calcium 150 ppm; silica 58 ppm; fluoride 3.5 ppm; iron 1,000 ppb; manganese 70 ppb; magnesium 38 ppb; zinc 10 ppb; phosphorous 0.05 ppb; selenium 0.05 ppb.

IRON SPRING

Alkalinity 1,644 mg/L; bicarbonate 1,644 mg/L; sodium, dissolved 811 mg/L; hardness 464 mg/L; chloride 438 mg/L; sulfate 228 mg/L; calcium, dissolved 79 mg/L; magnesium, dissolved 65 mg/L; potassium, dissolved 60 mg/L; fluoride 1.0 mg/L; lithium, dissolved 0.96 mg/L; iron, dissolved 0.79 mg/L; nitrate, dissolved 0.07 mg/L; nitrate/nitrite 0.07 mg/L; barium, dissolved 0.04 mg/L; arsenic, dissolved 0.001 mg/L.

LITHIA SPRING

Sodium, dissolved 2,300 mg/L; alkalinity 2,242 mg/L; bicarbonate 2,174 mg/L; chloride 1,360 mg/L; sulfate 589 mg/L; hardness 144 mg/L; potassium, dissolved 125 mg/L; magnesium, dissolved 29 mg/L; calcium, dissolved 10 mg/L; lithium, dissolved 3.70 mg/L; fluoride 3.3 mg/L; arsenic, dissolved 0.114 mg/L; barium, dissolved 0.03 mg/L.

Facing page: Enjoy a private soak in your own hot springs pool at Antero Hot Springs Cabins.
STEWART M. GREEN

Glenwood Canyon is the scenic site for Glenwood Hot Springs Resort. STEWART M. GREEN

ORVIS HOT SPRINGS
Sulfur 1,130–1,200 mg/L; calcium 280–305 mg/L; potassium 34.1–36.3 mg/L; magnesium 19.4–21 mg/L; fluorine 4.20–4.44 mg/L; lithium 1.67–1.71 mg/L; manganese 0.010–0.147 mg/L.

OVERLOOK HOT SPRINGS SPA
Sulfates/sulfur 14,000 mg/L; sodium 790 mg/L; chloride 180 mg/L; silica 54 mg/L; magnesium 25 mg/L; potassium 25 mg/L; fluoride 4.3 mg/L; lithium 2.9 mg/L; boron 1.8 mg/L; arsenic 0.12 mg/L; iron 0.08 mg/L; zinc 0.01 mg/L.

SALIDA HOT SPRINGS AQUATIC CENTER
Bicarbonate 223.1 ppm; sulphate 207.4 ppm; sodium 108.5 ppm; chloride 54.7 ppm; silica 54.1 ppm; calcium 19.7 ppm; potassium 16.5 ppm; aluminum iron oxide 1.7 ppm.

SODA SPRING
Alkalinity 1,020 mg/L; bicarbonate 1,020 mg/L; sodium, dissolved 702 mg/L; chloride 378 mg/L; hardness 269 mg/L; sulfate 196 mg/L; calcium, dissolved 24 mg/L; magnesium, dissolved 51 mg/L; iron, dissolved 1.96 mg/L; fluoride 1.0 mg/L; lithium, dissolved 0.85 mg/L; potassium, dissolved 0.53 mg/L; nitrate, dissolved 0.46 mg/L; nitrate/nitrite 0.46 mg/L; barium, dissolved 0.04 mg/L.

THE SPRINGS RESORT & SPA
Sulfate 1,400 mg/L; sodium 790 mg/L; chloride 180 mg/L; potassium 90 mg/L; silica 54 mg/L; magnesium 25 mg/L; fluoride 4.3 mg/L; lithium 2.9 mg/L; boron 1.8 mg/L; manganese 0.23 mg/L; arsenic 0.12 mg/L; iron 0.08 mg/L; zinc 0.01 mg/L.

STEAMBOAT SPRING
Sodium, dissolved 2,470 mg/L; alkalinity 2,454 mg/L; bicarbonate 2,454 mg/L; chloride 1,470 mg/L; sulfate 628 mg/L; hardness 187 mg/L; potassium, dissolved 130 mg/L; magnesium, dissolved 31 mg/L; calcium, dissolved 24 mg/L; lithium, dissolved 3.75 mg/L; fluoride 3.5 mg/L; arsenic, dissolved 0.110 mg/L; barium, dissolved 0.03 mg/L.

SULPHUR CAVE SPRING
Sodium, dissolved 2,220 mg/L; alkalinity 1,340 mg/L; bicarbonate 1,340 mg/L; chloride 1,300 mg/L; sulfate 836 mg/L; hardness 204 mg/L; potassium, dissolved 120 mg/L; magnesium, dissolved 32 mg/L; calcium, dissolved 29 mg/L; lithium, dissolved 3.45 mg/L; fluoride 3.2 mg/L; arsenic, dissolved 0.099 mg/L; barium, dissolved 0.04 mg/L; iron, dissolved 0.03 mg/L; nitrite, dissolved 0.01 mg/L.

SULPHUR SPRING
Alkalinity 2,390 mg/L; bicarbonate 2,390 mg/L; sodium, dissolved 2,010 mg/L; chloride 1,250 mg/L; sulfate 584 mg/L; hardness 235 mg/L; potassium, dissolved 120 mg/L; magnesium, dissolved 36 mg/L; calcium, dissolved 35 mg/L; fluoride 3.4 mg/L; lithium, dissolved 3.35 mg/L; arsenic, dissolved 0.087 mg/L; barium, dissolved 0.02 mg/L; cadmium, dissolved 0.006 mg/L.

SUNWATER SPA
Alkalinity 1,310 mg/L; calcium 303 mg/L; sodium 159 mg/L; sulfate 96.7 mg/L; chloride 96.4 mg/L; magnesium 82.6 mg/L; silica 22 mg/L; potassium 19.5 mg/L; fluoride 0.64 mg/L; iron 0.54 mg/L; zinc 0.34 mg/L; lithium 0.277 mg/L.

TRIMBLE SPA & NATURAL HOT SPRINGS
Sulfate 1,180 mg/L; calcium 417 mg/L; sodium 363 mg/L; chloride 183 mg/L; chlorine 84 mg/L; silica 59.6 mg/L; manganese 33 mg/L; potassium 32.4 mg/L; magnesium 28.8 mg/L; fluoride 2.5 mg/L; iron 2.5 mg/L; lithium 1.238 mg/L; boron 1.2 mg/L; ortho-phosphate 0.25 mg/L; arsenic 0.192 mg/L; zinc 0.008 mg/L; mercury <1.0002 mg/L; cadmium 0 mg/L; nitrate/nitrite as nitrogen 0 mg/L; phosphate 0 mg/L; selenium 0 mg/L.

WIESBADEN HOT SPRINGS
Sulfate 1,015.8 mg/L; calcium 383.3 mg/L; sodium 81.0 mg/L; silica 52.3 mg/L; potassium 45.0 mg/L; bicarbonate 37.4 mg/L; magnesium 11.1 mg/L; lithium 1.1 mg/L.

INDEX

The Mother Spring is the deepest hot spring in the world. STEWART M. GREEN

ABOUT THE AUTHOR

Susan Joy Paul is a freelance writer, hiker, climber, soaker, and mountaineer, and the coauthor of *Touring Colorado Hot Springs*, 2nd edition (2012) and author of *Hiking Waterfalls in Colorado* (2013) and *Climbing Colorado's Mountains* (2016). When she's not exploring the backcountry or writing books, Susan likes to drink beer, eat plants, and watch the grass grow. She lives in Colorado Springs, Colorado.

The author relaxes between hot springs soaks. PHOTO BY DOUG HATFIELD